Great Dramas of the Bible

By William Earle Cameron

Unity Books
Unity Village, Missouri

We gratefully acknowledge the following artists and photographers for their contributions to this book:

Shyrlee Barnaby Cover
Ewing Galloway First Photograph;
    38; 64; 90; 148; 176; 238; 252
Garry Hood 26
Evan Lattimer 76
Cindy Salans Rosenheim 52
Betty Chaisson 204

CONTENTS

Introduction

This is your opportunity to share in human-kind's greatest adventure—an epic journey through the "Great Dramas of the Bible." This book follows a historical procession in the saga of humanity's evolving awareness of God.

The Bible is the most instructive history we possess, for it is truly the story of each one of us. From beginning to end, the teachings of the Scriptures can reveal the truths of our own potential and guide us individually in learning and growing and becoming what God intends us to be. All the great portrayals of characters in the Bible have their counterparts in each of us, and their dramatic impact can be brought right into our minds and hearts. The Bible is your story. Its dramas are unfinished; they await your recognition to become a powerful and exciting influence in the greatest adventure you can ever know—the evolution of your own spiritual nature.

Great Dramas of the Bible

Abraham—Father of Believers

We are going to accompany Abraham on his original journey of faith toward the Promised Land—first through the ancient Bible lands of 4,000 years ago, and then within you, in the interior journey of your own soul growth.

Abram had been his name in the beginning; he was the son of Terah. It was Terah who had received the first inspiration to leave the old city of Ur in the Euphrates Valley (the capital of a great civilization, rich in tangibles and culture, but steeped in idolatry and morally and spiritually impoverished). Terah had led his family as far as the Oasis of Haran, but there he was content to settle down again. After Terah died, when Abram was seventy-five years old, he received the call: . . . *Get thee out of thy country* . . . (Gen. 12:1 A.V.) and he went out not knowing his destination. But, he knew what he was looking for— . . . *a city which has foundations, whose builder and maker is God,* (Heb. 11:10) which is the Hebrew way of saying that he was looking for a new spiritual life based on the foundation of truth of one God, one Power and Presence.

Before Abraham, there had been no feeling of belonging to God. But with Abram's acceptance of God's "travel orders," the foundation was laid

1

for a covenant (a partnership agreement) between God and man, upon which three great religions of the future would be based.

The Bible reports simply that Abram left the Oasis of Haran with his wife Sarai and his nephew Lot, and he arrived at Canaan. It was a hard journey of 300 miles from Haran to Canaan, however, and it must have taken weeks. Like our American pioneers, they entered a land that was already inhabited and they were generally not warmly welcomed. Every tribe had its own gods, and images were proudly displayed. Tribesmen were ready to fight at the sight of other god-like images. Abram's way must have been made much easier because his God was invisible.

Upon reaching Canaan, Abram erected altars at Shechem and Bethel. He went south, and because of drought and famine he soon abandoned the Promised Land and went . . . *down to Egypt* . . . (Gen. 12:10) a country much like the one he originally left.

Because he feared what might happen to him, he asked the beautiful Sarai to pretend to be his sister. She was taken into Pharaoh's house to live; and as her "brother," Abram was honored and rewarded with many herds, servants, and possessions. But we read in the story that the Lord plagued Pharaoh because of his *affaire d'amour* with Sarai; and although Pharaoh was quite angry at Abram for not telling him that Sarai was really his wife, apparently wanting no more trouble with their God, he sent Abraham away intact with his wife and all his new possessions. Upon their return to Bethel, now quite wealthy, strife broke out between Abram's and Lot's herdsmen and they decided to separate. Here Abram did something remarkable (almost unheard of in those days, for, as the older man, he had prior claim to everything): in the spirit of high-minded generosity, he gave Lot first choice! Lot took advantage of his uncle and chose the land that seemed to be far richer and greener, but he overlooked one thing— the presence of a certain people who lived in a city called Sodom.

You probably remember how Lot's wife, in disobedience, "looked back" and turned into a pillar of salt as Sodom was being destroyed. From then on everything went downhill for Lot. He eventually had to be rescued from invaders by Abram. For this gallantry, and for doing the best he could to save Sodom, Abram became full leader and was honored by Melchizedek, a very important character in the Bible. Lot, on the other hand, lost everything and became a fugitive.

Abram and Sarai were then renamed. In the Bible a name always refers to a person's nature. Abram, which meant *high father of a tribe,* became Abraham, *father of multitudes.* Sarai, meaning *contentious, quarrelsome,* became Sarah, *princess, mellow, noble lady.* Their expanding faith had reached a point where it could move mountains, and anything can happen with such faith. Yet they couldn't quite accept the miracle that had been promised to follow—a challenge certainly, to anyone's faith—a couple, almost one hundred years old, to have a child! So when the Lord told them this, Abraham and Sarah laughed!

Abraham decided to do what seemed the obvious thing to do—he had a son, Ishmael, by Sarah's handmaid, Hagar. But eventually, through angelic inspiration, they were both convinced that the impossible could happen, and they had their son. They named him "God laughed"—Isaac. There was one sad note: Sarah, worried about heirship for her son, convinced Abraham to cast Ishmael and his mother out of the tribe. They, however, were well cared for by God.

Lastly in this story came Abraham's great moment of faith when he believed that he was called upon to sacrifice his son Isaac. The story is loaded with emotion and drama. Abraham believed he was asked to make a burnt offering of his only child, whose birth was a miracle and whom he must have dearly loved. And the young boy—so trusting—followed his father up the mountain, innocently asking where the sacrificial lamb was. It

4

was only at the last moment, his hand raised with a dagger, that Abraham realized this wasn't required of him.

This is a classic example of the Bible storyteller's way of going to great extremes to get a point across. In this case, it was to show that God must be trusted implicitly. The Bible compilers also used it as a teaching point against the practice of sacrifice, a primitive custom that all the prophets were against; and they were shown in this early story that God doesn't want our possessions but our hearts. Anyway, it ended happily. Abraham lived a blessed life to a ripe old age. Isaac became the second patriarch, and even Ishmael became the founder of a mighty people, the Arab nation. Abraham had truly become the father of believers, the father of all who believe in the reality of one living God and who follow and trust the divine urge that calls each of us to reach out for the spiritual life. He is the symbol of the great quest of all our souls for their Source. Just as the Bible is the epic story of God's nature unfolding in the life of man, the story of Abram becoming Abraham is the story of the activity of faith in us—starting us on our path of spiritual growth and refinement.

The story may or may not be completely historically accurate; but it is true, for it is typical of the inward spiritual experience any of us have when we step out on faith. And it reveals the principles and pitfalls of the beginnings and the continual expansion process involved in working with faith and developing our spiritual consciousness—the Promised Land.

All of us receive "calls" from God. Many are subtle, almost constant, and often undiscerned and unheeded. Occasionally, the calls are quite dramatic—sudden, powerful, life-changing experiences that point us toward our destiny.

I heard a story that seems incredible, yet is a fairly typical "call from God." The story is about another Abraham—Abraham Lincoln. It happened in New Salem, Illinois. Abe and his partner Berry were on the porch of their little store discussing their failing business. Berry asked: "How much longer do you think we can keep going?" Abe answered, "It looks like our business has about winked out." And then he continued, "You know, I wouldn't mind so much if I could just do what I want to do. I want to study law. I wouldn't mind so much if we could sell everything we've got and pay all our bills and have enough left over to buy one book, 'Blackstone's Commentary on English Law'; but I guess I can't." About that time a strange-looking wagon came up the road. The driver drove close to the porch and the man looked up at Abraham Lincoln and said: "I'm trying to move my family West, and I'm out of money. I've a good barrel on here and I could sell

6

it for fifty cents." Lincoln's eyes went along the wagon and came to the man's wife, who looked up at him pleadingly, her face thin and emaciated; and Abraham Lincoln put his hand in his pocket and took out, according to him, "the last fifty cents I had," and he said, "I reckon I could use a good barrel." All day long the barrel sat on the porch; Berry kept chiding him about it. Late in the evening Abe walked out, looked down into the barrel and saw something at the bottom—papers he hadn't noticed before. His long arm went down into them and rumpled them around, and he hit something solid. He pulled out a book and stood petrified. It was the "Commentary on English Law," by Blackstone.

Now, these are his words: "I stood there holding the book, looking up toward the heavens. There came a deep impression on me that God had something for me to do—and He was showing me now that I had to get ready for it. Why this miracle otherwise?"

That day God touched the heart of Abraham Lincoln, and his life blazed out in glory to do the thing that God needed to be doing in the United States of America. That's the way spiritual journeys often start—from a book, an idea, an awakening. . . . *Get thee out of thy country.* . . . (Gen. 12:1 A.V.) "Look up! God has something for you to do!" Although in looking back we some-

7

times discover that preceding that lasting impression, represented by Abram's faith in God, there was a parent inspiration represented by Terah, Abram's father—an urge for something higher which we perhaps followed for a short time and then forgot and settled back into the old ways.

We can begin to see how the underlying truths of the Bible are often concealed in biblical names. The Abram traits are quite human. Even after he discovered God's infinite intelligence and power as the very personal help in every need, and trusted in God for guidance and inspiration, he made mistakes. He left the Promised Land soon after he arrived for the old material securities of Egypt during the time of drought and famine. He, rather cowardly, disowned his wife and let another man take her. And after a lot of proof of God's power in his life, he still laughed at God's promise to him of a son of his own. Even the notion of sacrifice was something out of his own subconscious, for this is completely out of harmony with the character of God. And surely Abram had other plans for himself when God called. He was probably well off. He may have been fairly secure where he was, and his life was undoubtedly upset by going off into a strange new land. How typical! For this is the way rebirth happens to us—inside. As spiritual aspirants we reenact the whole epic story of Abraham in our inner lives.

When we receive the Abram inspiration, we will experience all the elements of this marvelous story. There will be times of exalted states of mind, fruitful and prolific as the Oasis of Haran. We will, nevertheless, still wrangle with our as yet contentious, unregenerated emotions (Sarai) and our unremitting negative thoughts (Lot). There will be droughts and famines—dry periods in which we can no longer seem to remain inspired or are even afraid to really trust the inspiration we have already received—times in which even our most fervent prayers seem unanswered. And we will be tempted to go back down into the seemingly reliable old worldly beliefs (Egypt), which always draw us right back into the same old bondage. We may indeed, at some time, abandon our high callings and allow the ruling materialistic mentality (Pharaoh) to entirely take over our emotions.

But this is wonderful to remember: God's Spirit in us can rescue us from any of our mistakes and failures, redeem our emotions, help us honorably and nobly part company with our Lot-type thoughts and establish us in righteousness (the blessing of Melchizedek).

With spiritual growth there will come a time when our uplifted thoughts and feelings will actually alter our nature. We will receive a new name—and the promise of a son of our own, the birth into our human nature of our true spiritual nature. Even then there may be tendencies to feel that in working with God it would somehow appease Him if we sacrificed the glorious Truth of our spiritual identity. But we will find that we are not to give this up, and this is the very realization that allows God to bring forth His divine heritage for us, through us. And we will learn, as did Abraham, that the only sacrifice God ever wants from us is our hearts—to give up the lesser so that He can add the greater. When we sacrifice the "ram" (the butt-headed notions that disclaim the estate of our spiritual birthright), and when we give up those concepts that separate us from God, He will somehow tell us, "This is my child, in whom I am well pleased."

In spiritual growth there are many "promised lands." Each new state of spiritual awareness is filled with the good of God, just what we need when we need it. For this reason more Bible Truth is caught than taught, and the marvel of the Bible is that each story lesson is capable of revealing level after level of new, progressive, living inspiration and guidance. If you possess a good basic understanding of the Bible, then it will always be there when you need it.

If you understand the deeper implications of the story of Abraham, you will know many important truths about your spiritual unfoldment. You will

10

know that you have within you the invincible power of God's Spirit, that there is within you that which always knows what is highest and best, and can do all things—lawfully, lovingly, and divinely. You will know there is nothing too hard for the Spirit of God in you to overcome. And you will know that God-in-you comes forth more and more powerfully, efficiently, and effectually as you trust in His promises and center your faith in the principles and plans that He provides for a divine partnership in your life.

Is your indwelling God coming forth and growing in your nature? Are His promises coming true in your life? We all need that spirit of Abraham, father of believers, who proved that . . . *he who is in you is greater than he who is in the world.* (I John 4:4)

The Trinity Formula—
Infinite and Intimate

Oscar Wilde said: *One's real life is seldom the one we have.* We rarely suspect what our life could be. To look at it another way, a man from the Midwest put an ad in a newspaper which read: *I am 58 years old. Would like to marry a young woman of 30—who has a tractor. Please send picture of tractor.* Life holds so much more than most of us find in it.

Charles Fillmore said: *All the powers that are attributed to God may become operative in man.* Each of us is a masterpiece of creation. Only the infinite, universal, miraculous intelligence and power of God could have created and produced you. We are all made from the best—from God Himself. We are the image and likeness of God, with one notable exception: we come into life not knowing this, therefore, with the problem of finding out who we truly are. As a result, life can be a most confusing experience.

When we don't really know the potential of our spiritual heritage, we can get into all sorts of trouble, and like the farmer, we can become so absorbed in our little, gross, sense-bound world and so settled down in it that we cannot perceive anything beyond it. We don't notice; we don't care;

we don't imagine; we never really discover what life means.

This was also brought very close to home in the great American tragedy, "Death of a Salesman." The salesman, Willie Loman, had been taught, and he tried to teach his sons, that the goal in life was to try to get ahead of the next fellow. But as he got old and was cast into the ash can by changing policies of his company, he committed suicide. At the grave one son said: *"He had a good dream to come out 'number one'."* But the other son perceived beyond the confusion of these temporary earthbound values and said: *"He never knew who he was."*

We all perceive this to some degree and we call it a "tragedy." The idea of tragedy implies a profound respect for the essential importance of a man and of what he can be. It implies purpose and meaning, even if it can only be seen as growth toward some concealed destiny. We all are more than ourselves. Our main job in life is to constantly go beyond what we now are. The overall principle for the transcending growth possible with all people can be found in the concept of the Trinity, which we most likely know as the Father, Son, and Holy Spirit.

If we are indeed the spiritual image and likeness of God, then it is our privilege, our responsibility, and our destiny to put the infinite nature and powers of God to work in our lives. Jesus tells us these are all found within us: " . . . *the kingdom of God is in the midst of you."* (Luke 17:21) But to discover them, intimately within, we have to first understand the relationship that exists between God of the infinite and ourselves. The ancient sages told us to "know thyself," a key to the full life.

The best way to know ourselves is to know God—our heavenly Father. From the beginning we have always attempted to do this. In the Bible we find people searching for God from the first to the last page.

Part of the real challenge for any religion is to formulate a good way to think about God. By His very nature, God is infinite, absolute, omnipotent, omnipresent, and omniscient. We, in our three-dimensional human understanding, are not able to comprehend the totality of God. We must first attempt our definitions and understanding of Him in man-sized images. In the Old Testament, the most advanced concept of God is given in the very beginning (the first chapter in Genesis), which was placed first because it provides a good metaphysical introduction of God as the spiritual First Cause, original Creator and Sustainer of the universe. In the very next chapter, concepts are reduced to a more mundane interpretation in which God is portrayed as an anthropomorphic image of man with some of our own less desirable human traits, such as jealousy, wrath, and a tendency toward vengeance and punishment.

We tend to attribute to God what we are at any level, and conversely, we tend to be what we think God is. As our concept of God grows, we evolve into it. The greatest contribution of the Hebrew religion was the idea they evolved that there is one God. From Abraham on, the Jews believed in but one God. There was, however, a great deal of latitude as to His charcteristics and attributes, and often they were far more human than divine. Early in Hebrew history and in their more primitive conceptions of God, He was to them a tribal God, a bearded storm God, a national war God, a God that could be fierce, revengeful, but also a friend, a confidant or partner. The relationship between a Jew and his God was sometimes stringent, possessive, protective, exclusive, at times exasperative and often warm, encouraging, and rewarding.

Our concepts of God have evolved since then. Jesus revealed our highest, most transcending concept: God is love. Love is the essence and totality of God's nature. It was for love that He created the world; it is by love that He sustains it; and it is in love that we best relate to God our indwelling Father and closest relative. Jesus' mission was to consciously reunite us with God, in spirit and truth. But, for good reasons, Christians came to worship Jesus Himself as God, or an extension of God. The ministry of Jesus, with His strange and wonderful powers, was "divine"—a direct revelation of the fullness of God in a man. And there was yet another divine dimension that was introduced through Jesus: the Comforter, the Teacher, the enduring, empowering Spirit of Truth. As with the person of Jesus, the activity of the Holy Spirit awed the early Christians too much not to revere and worshipfully venerate it. The worship of Christ and the Holy Spirit put the early Christians at odds with the Jews and the First Commandment of the Mosaic Law, which demanded that God alone shall be worshipped. But, because of their new experience, the followers of Jesus couldn't say all they wanted to say about God in traditional Judaism. They eventually solved their problem by "perceiving a mystery" wherein God is comprised of three entities. This was an enrichment and a broadening in the evolution of man's idea about God, which gives great insight into understanding the nature and the ways of God.

The church doctrine of the Holy Trinity has an interesting history. The Bible itself doesn't mention the term *trinity*, but it often implies that the Supreme Being is one God in three centers of consciousness (seen in three aspects). The outline of the doctrine began with the contact between early followers of Jesus Christ and the Hellenistic philosophy, which attempted to explain Christianity in terms of metaphysics with such metaphysical concepts as the *Logos, the Divine Word* that is found in the writings of John. A long time later (after much controversy among theologians) the final orthodox version of the Trinity, in which God is regarded as three *persons,* was accepted at the Nicene Council and again at the second Council of Constantinople. This formula, which the theologians said was "above reason" and not demonstrable by logic or scriptural proof, was used to instruct and supervise converts, and to sum up the church's teaching about God, Jesus Christ, and the Holy Spirit. The concept of *Person* was often considered confusing and contradictory, and the controversies continued for centuries—resulting sometimes in conflicts, splits, and some very un-Christlike use of force—finally giving rise to the Unitarian movement (no connection with Unity School of Christianity).

But the unfortunate religious history of the doctrine of the Trinity doesn't negate its value as a basic formula to help us reach a higher understanding of the totality of God. The term *Father* gives us a cosmic grasp of God as universal Parent-Spirit—the originating First Cause, Prime Source, Infinite Intelligence, and Ultimate Essence of all creation above and beyond all time and space. The *Son* is that which is begotten by the Father, like the Father in nature and quality, an expression in time and space of what the Father is in essence. (Jesus often talked about it in terms of *seeds*, the perfect pattern for perfect expression: *"You, therefore, must be perfect as your heavenly Father is perfect."*) (Matt. 5:48) The *Holy Spirit* is God in motion, the operation of the original creative power in the individual, the specific spiritual activity of God within, rather than apart from man.

We need to identify with and learn to participate in the great cosmic creative process by which God expresses Himself and brings forth His good into the world. Einstein provided a paramount breakthrough in our awareness of universal oneness and helped usher in a new era of living with his concise triune formula, $E = MC^2$, restating the trinity idea of source, pattern, and motion in the scientific perception of one universal energy expressing itself in everything in various degrees of participation, varying only in its rate of motion (vibration).

Charles Fillmore translated the *Father, Son, Holy Spirit* trinity into a very workable formula of *mind, idea, and expression,* a concept that helps us relate the way God creatively "thinks out" His universe to our own creative mind process and our individual ability to use this process and working power in developing our own lives.

As God's children, His threefold nature is complemented in us. We are Spirit, soul, and body, and we must understand our threefold being relationship with God—and within ourselves—for optimum soul growth unfoldment. The important thing is to learn to translate the Infinite into the intimate and bring our lives into line with the original creative power.

The Bible often regards man in a threefold nature. Jesus' concern was always with the whole person. He never lost sight of any of these three areas, and His approach therefore was always personal—intimate. But, I would like now to return to an Old Testament story to demonstrate the Trinity as a "formula for soul growth," and a pattern for the unfolding of consciousness.

The story is about three persons: Jacob, his twin brother Esau, and the man that Jacob became, Israel. Jacob and Esau were grandsons of Father Abraham. Jacob became the third patriarch. (Their father was the second patriarch Isaac, and their mother was Rebekah.) Esau had actually been born first, which gave him the firstborn rights of family name, the ruler of the clan, a double share of the father's fortune, and in this case heritage to the spiritual lineage as patriarch. These things, however, meant little to Esau, a rough, hairy, earthy type. But Jacob, a more refined type, valued the birthright; and it is said that he even struggled in their mother's womb to be first—hence, he was named Jacob, which means "supplanter." Later, in a moment of hunger after a hunting trip, Esau bargained away his birthright to Jacob for a bowl of pottage. And again afterward, in connivance with his mother Rebekah, Jacob managed to deceive his aged, nearly blind father Isaac into again giving him the birthright by putting on a hairy goatskin so that he felt like his hairy brother Esau. From that day on he was compelled to live under the threat of his brother's anger. With his mother's help, however, he was able to escape and return to Haran, the land of his ancestors.

The first night away from home, he fell asleep with his head on a rock and dreamed of angels going up and down a ladder; and he heard God's voice from the top renewing the promise He had made to Abraham—a new understanding and an assurance of God's continual presence. It made him realize that, even in the worst circumstance, *"Surely the Lord is in this place; and I did not know it."* (Gen. 28:16)

After this original spiritual experience Jacob continued on to Haran where he lived many years with his Uncle Laban. He also continued his struggle in life, mostly with his uncle. He worked seven years as a shepherd in order to wed Uncle Laban's beautiful daughter Rachel, only to find out on his wedding night that he had been tricked into marrying her older sister Leah. He then worked seven more years for Rachel. During his stay in Haran he had twelve sons, who became the founders of the twelve tribes of Israel. Eventually, Jacob managed to trick his uncle in a cattle deal; Jacob then left for his original home with all his family and possessions; his uncle chased and caught him, and they finally arrived at a personal covenant: " . . . *The Lord watch between you and me, when we are absent one from the other.*" (Gen. 31:49)

As Jacob approached Canaan, he became almost panic-stricken about facing his estranged brother Esau. The night before their meeting he had another dream and a second spiritual experience in which he wrestled with an angel (within himself), and he persisted in the inner struggle until he was rewarded with a blessing. This experience brought forth a new nature in Jacob, a new name, "Israel," which means Prince of God, or the awareness of being a Son of God.

It turned out that, after all his worries, his brother Esau was glad to see him. Jacob was able to settle for a long time in his original home of Canaan. Finally he moved his tribe to Egypt during a drought, at the invitation of Joseph.

Within this story we see the formula of spiritual evolution at work in the threefold nature of man, and we witness the striking transformation by which Jacob is developed into a spiritual man.

Esau represents the level of consciousness in which we are sense-bound: a level that judges by appearances, lives and attains things by force, and centers its attention on physical needs and gratification. This is the "first born" in all of us. It is natural for us to first consider ourselves physical humans and to look to and depend upon physical and human resources.

Jacob represents us at our more cultured, intellectual, reflective level of consciousness. Here especially we discover the mental laws of cause and effect, which usurp the birthright of Esau with new control and mastery over our bodies and our environments, for such is the power of mental energy or action over the physical plane of existence.

Esau and Jacob live and vie in each of us. The intellect always seeks to overcome the physical and the material, but because of the many complex, conflicting drives and frustrations resulting from our inner struggles, the mental is always bound to the physical until it becomes spiritual.

When we place ourselves completely under the action of our thoughts and their consequences, our advancement is always hindered. But if we place ourselves above our thoughts by centering ourselves in spiritual interests (as Jesus said, " . . . *worship the Father in spirit and truth* . . . "), (John 4:23) our minds become gateways to higher consciousness. It is here that Spirit comes into the picture, inspiring us and lifting us to new heights of awareness.

This spiritual experience of new awareness (rebirth) is "Israel," a breakthrough into spiritual consciousness in which " . . . *behold, the new has come"* (II Cor. 5:17)—we ascend the Jacob's ladder of our spiritual progression, and we live from a new level of being in which more of God's infinite intelligence, power, and purpose can find higher expression through us.

Remember, Jacob changed, Esau didn't. But Esau defers only to our spiritual nature. We never succeed in intellectually fighting it out with our lower nature. Often, however, one brief spiritual experience can transcend the laws of both our physical and mental natures and bring a blessing into our problems and difficulties for the rest of our lives—if we persist in supporting this inspiration and vision with our thoughts and prayers.

We all have individual lives within a greater life. Our main job in life is to go beyond where we now are. To do this we need to constantly cultivate a state of intellectual consciousness that invites and introduces into our lives a spiritual influence that lifts us up and takes us beyond where we are—into higher levels of our own being—and gives us a "new name," a new nature.

Jacob's transformation is an inspiration to all of us to learn to place ourselves over our thoughts, to aim our thoughts where we want to be. Anytime we lift up our thoughts in prayer we are seeking God's infinite support. Each of us must find it for ourselves within ourselves, within the framework of the Trinity formula for creative soul growth.

Think in terms of attributes, those of God that can be expressed by us. Identify the quality you need, personally, intimately, with the unlimited equivalent divine attribute as it exists in God's nature. Especially in prayer, if you need health, affirm divine life; if you need order, affirm divine order; and if you need love and forgiveness, affirm divine love. If you need prosperity, affirm your oneness with God's infinite abundant ideas; and in all of these learn to hold your attention fast and true to these infinite qualities of God.

Know that such a God lives in you—intimately—as the divine Source, and as a personal, all-wise, infinitely loving Father who knows and cares and will work in you with His nature and His power to fulfill all those purposes in your life which were His for you from the very beginning and which constitute your real life.

Putting Evil in Its Place

After hearing a gloomy newscast, a man said: "Isn't the world terrible?" Someone replied: "Which one?" This gives us an important insight: To know something is not to be bound by it. Perhaps this is the distinction between a metaphysician and one who isn't. The nonmetaphysician tends to assume that life, as he knows it, is permanent. The metaphysician learns to see through that which *now is* to that which *can be*. Unity teaches the higher vision. We cultivate the art of seeing the invisible, of looking beyond and above the temporal to the potential. We learn to center ourselves in the unseen—the realm of spiritual powers, principles, and resources that can bring all things right, and, in the process, put evil in its place.

What is evil's place in the scheme of things? The question of good and evil has perplexed theologians and philosophers through the ages, and it is still a major issue in religious doctrines. Many churches are obsessed with "original sin," "Adam's fall," and an overshadowing concern with evil. A true understanding of good and evil will help us to better understand all of life and will also give us a working knowledge on how to render evil ineffective.

27

The Bible is our great written heritage of spiritual knowledge. Its immense value, in part, is that it doesn't just set down ultimate information in compact formulas, or it would very likely be a short and concise book. Instead, it is an epic book of life that reveals its Truth progressively through a wide variation of plots and dramas that cover every theme in human experience. Each story, in some marvelous way, relates eternal Truth to each of us, right where we are, inspiring and guiding us each according to our individual needs and our present level of understanding. The Bible, therefore, gives us not only spiritual knowledge, but an all-important perspective.

Three basic views of good and evil that appear in the Bible progressively meet different levels of human needs and understanding. Two views are found in the Old Testament, which is the original Jewish Bible. One is originally Jewish, and the other was borrowed by the Jews. The first view is the Genesis story of the fall of Adam and Eve, which says that, by eating the fruit of the tree of knowledge of good and evil, they disobeyed God; and, as a result of their own misdeed, they brought evil into the world. The second view developed gradually as a result of the Jews' experiences as a nation, rather than as individuals. Throughout their history, the Hebrews were almost continuously dominated by pagan powers:

the Assyrians, Babylonians, Persians, Egyptians, Syrians, and Romans. One after the other, these empires ruled the Jews. Naturally, to the Jews, because they understood themselves to be God's "chosen people," it came to appear that the world was ruled not by God but by pagan empires. The Jews had a long contact in captivity with Babylon and the religion of the Persians called Zoroastrianism, and it supplied a view as to the nature of the universe which seemed to match and explain the Jewish experience. According to this view the world is a "battleground" between two opposite spiritual forces. They believed that at the head of the evil forces stood a god of evil. The Persian magi said that at some future day God would destroy the evil forces and eliminate them from the world. Then, freed from the activities of evil, the world would be a good and happy place to live. The sacred books of Zoroastrianism taught that, following the destruction of the "evil one," the dead would be raised and judged, the wicked would be punished, and the righteous would enter into and enjoy a new age. More and more as the Jews meditated on their national fortune, this seemed to supply the explanation they sought.

In the development of Jewish thought, as their world outlook became definitely pessimistic, the Persian concept of dualism underwent some changes, and there evolved out of all this a great

Messianic hope. It had two elements: a national vindication for the Jews by the overthrow of their opponents and the restoration of the kingdom of David, and a supernatural cosmic victory over all evil with the establishment of God's universal kingship, or the kingdom of God. This then became Jesus' central theme—the kingdom of God. And in spite of the fact that over and over He emphasized that His kingdom is within, almost everyone—the Jews, and later, the Christians— assumed that He was still referring to the old Jewish-Persian version and its preoccupation with the "battle" between the forces of good and evil. After the time of Jesus, Augustine enacted the doctrine of "original sin" (to include even newborn children), which was never mentioned in the Bible. It was Milton's "Paradise Lost" that crystallized our present concepts of hell and damnation.

The third basic view of good and evil is found in the spiritual understanding of the teachings of Jesus, in which He said: *"You have heard that it was said, 'An eye for an eye and a tooth for a tooth,' But I say to you, Do not resist one who is evil. But if any one strikes you on the right cheek, turn to him the other also . . . ."* (Matt. 5:38, 39) Most people don't really believe that turning the other cheek works. We smile at its innocence.

If someone literally hit you on your right cheek and you literally turned your other cheek, they might not hit you back. It might make them realize that they were wrong and feel bad about it—and change their ways. But they might not. It might irritate them even more and they would hit you again—even harder; and if they did, it would not disprove Jesus' principle—because you would have missed the inner meaning, the deeper spiritual truth that Jesus was revealing in this illustration. Paul expressed it: *Do not be overcome by evil, but overcome evil with good.* (Rom. 12:21)

Jesus was proclaiming that the only way to overcome evil is with good, again reinforced by Paul's Scripture: *If God is for us, who is against us?* (Rom. 8:31) The principle is that there is only one Presence and Power, one Good in the universe—God.

We read in Genesis that God created everything (there is nothing in creation that did not come from God); and He pronounced it all good. Never has God withdrawn that pronouncement. There is still not a "bad" atom in the universe! Evil is a human production. Evil is not a thing; it is a function. It comes about by misuse, abuse, and nonuse. What we call evil exists only as a perversion of that which was created, and in essence remains, perfectly good. *Good* and *evil* are relative terms—interpretations from our human view of what we see, hear, and feel about anything in relation to the way it seems to affect us. They are highly subjective. Basically we name something good if we have dominion and authority over it, and we name it evil if it threatens us and seems beyond our power to control. The difference is truly in the eye of the beholder. Take electricity for example. For centuries it frightened people in the only form they knew, lightning. Now, under our control, it serves us in an amazing variety of beneficial ways. Occasionally, with misuse, it also injures or takes the life of someone; but this doesn't in any way render the marvelous force of electricity evil.

From the creation story, we learn that God is all, and all things are essentially good. Where do things go wrong? The cartoonist Walt Kelly once had Pogo say something classic: *"We has met the enemy, and they is us."* It is in us where the difference occurs: *"What comes out of a man is what defiles a man."* (Mark 7:20) It is the inherent powers for good that truly reside in all of us; but it's against natural law to believe in evil and produce good. We learn from the apple tree story of Eden that it is our negative view of life that gives evil the only power. The correction is also in us. It is the belief in both good and evil that needs to be healed. You are an original child of God, whom He pronounced "good," not "sinner." Yet, every man, woman, and child has the inborn freedom to choose at any time if he or she will support good

32

or evil. (Newborn children have a clean slate.) When "evil" appears because of our wrong choices and beliefs, we are also free at all times to withdraw our support.

Jesus' way of withdrawing support and putting evil in its place is by refusing to "eat" any more from the *tree of the knowledge of good and evil.* (Gen. 1:17) He admonished: "*. . . resist not evil.*" (Matt. 5:39 A.V.) It is practicing the opposite. It is giving active support and full attention to good, rather than fighting that which is less. *Good* is anything that fulfills us and God's plan for us. *Evil* is anything that diminishes us and thwarts His will. *Nonresistance* is the instruction to believe only in good. Nonresistance, as Paul said, is giving no *place to the devil.* (Eph. 4:27 A.V.) Nonresistance is a force for change that takes place within us, leading us in the way of God (the direction of good). To practice nonresistance is to learn to control and align the forces within ourselves with the spiritual influence possible under God's rulership in our lives, thereby letting Omnipresent Good express itself through us.

To know something is not to be bound by it. This is why Jesus taught us to return good for evil. The story of Eden is a poetic allegory about mankind's early emergence into reflective consciousness. It tells us, from a charming, childlike point of view, what it feels like to take on the privilege and responsibility of thinking as individuals with all the duties, problems, opportunities, and growing pains that are the fruition of choosing and "naming" things in our new life. Jesus was stating the corrective principle by which we can remedy the results of our wrong choices and misapplications of that which is basically good. He was disclosing the way to heal our wrong beliefs and sow new seeds—seeds that will harvest only good. It all happens in consciousness. Through nonresisting, we are no longer bound within; then the world changes. *"Resist not evil."* Instead, return good for evil. This is a universal, timeless principle.

In the Old Testament (in which we have been exploring for the basic principle of spiritual growth), Joseph, the fourth Patriarch, is an example of this principle—and a good one. Joseph was one of the youngest of twelve sons of Jacob. He was a sensitive, imaginative lad who, by his youthful vanity, irritated his older brothers so much that they sold him into slavery and had him carted off to Egypt. What could hurt more or give a young man better reason to be bitter, resentful, full of revenge, and think this is a terrible world than to have his own brothers do that? But Joseph didn't succumb to this kind of thinking. With his imaginative vision (symbolized by his coat of many colors), he looked past the so-called evil and let God (good) rule in his consciousness. He, therefore, was always in charge within himself. It didn't always prevent problems. He was falsely accused by his master's wife and landed in prison. But he still upheld the ideal that God was with him, and that God's basic goodness was at work in all things. Therefore, the influence of goodness, as leaven, worked through him, changing his character, establishing dominion and authority in his own inner world, and lifting him from his utterly unfortunate, adverse situation into the position of great power—second only to Pharaoh in command of all Egypt! And then, the dramatic climax to the whole story—his erring brothers stood before him, their hats in their hands, needing his help. And the man that Joseph had become found an easy, gratifying, rewarding, happy fruition to his whole life by forgiving and lovingly lavishing help upon his brothers. Do you remember how he stated the great principle? *"As for you, you meant evil against me; but God meant it for good. . . . "* (Gen. 50:20)

Through the principle of returning good for evil, a prisoner became a mighty prince. If Joseph had been an evil-fighter, he probably would never have gotten out of prison, and history might have been decided differently. Joseph proved the power of God (good) and it made him great. This is the way any person of spiritual understanding learns to act. The principle works any time, any place, and under any circumstance.

It has been proved over and over in the business world that the best thing to say when attacked with falsehood and slander is nothing. This is where the art of seeing the invisible becomes immensely important, because we often have to trust solely in the unseen principles and powers of Spirit and believe that they can make all things right. It is not an easy thing to do, but it pays big dividends.

Evil has no self-originating power. It borrows its only existence from our misconceptions of the ever-present goodness of God's creation. Jesus, whose supreme virtue was goodness, had a single eye to the good. And we read: *For the Son of God, Jesus Christ . . . was not Yes and No; but in Him it is always Yes. For all the promises of God find their Yes in Him.* (II Cor. 1:19, 20) We have His word and examples for it; fighting evil does not work.

What happens to us when we persist in eating from the wrong tree of knowledge? A farmer made a daily inspection of his apple bin and when he found an apple "going bad," he ate it. He spent his whole life eating rotten apples. When we spend our lives seeking out an opposing evil, that becomes the self-imposed confinement in which we experience life.

The infinite, enduring, inviolable truth and

goodness of God's creation does not need our paltry, self-righteous defense; it requires only our loving support. Those who are going to turn our world around, those who are going to become part of the answer rather than more of the problem, are those who really learn to work with the spiritual forces of nonresistance, turning evil back into good. The critical eye, the "isn't-the-world-terrible" viewpoint still prevails; and precious few yet possess the understanding use of Jesus' great corrective principle of active goodness that puts evil in its place. This higher vision, this "single eye," therefore, is now a sacred trust.

Your life is full of opportunities to practice the single eye and learn to elevate all your responses and choices toward Joseph's vantage point of truth that can affirm always: *God means things for good.* And by having that mind . . . *in you, which was also in Christ Jesus,* (Phil. 2:5 A.V.) let it be said that in you it is always yes.

The Mission of Moses

The Bible is the most instructive history we possess about the human predicament and how to deal with and successfully overcome the problems of being human. One of the greatest liberators in the Bible and of all time was Moses. Through Moses came the first five books of the Bible (called the Pentateuch), from which all of the teachings of Judaism and Christianity stem. Even the teachings of Jesus can be traced, verse by verse, to these five books of Moses.

The story of Moses and the Exodus is a wonderful, human story that leaves a lasting impression of how God's divine influence can work miracles through one man, and thereby lift multitudes out of the worst kind of bondage. The story is written in the eastern tradition of sometimes glorifying truth rather than fact; but it has more historical fact and less folklore than Genesis, for it isn't likely that a people would invent such a lowly origin for themselves as that of being unwanted slaves.

The story is solely about the children of Israel who had strayed away from the covenant of Father Abraham, drifted—as we all do, with bad habits—into a separation from God. Eventually they found themselves in intolerable bondage with little hope that it would ever improve. It is at this

39

crucial time that a great leader, Moses, rose among them. The story is like a three-act play, each act lasting "forty years" (the biblical symbol of whatever time it takes to properly fulfill something).

The setting of the first act is in Egypt, where the Jews have been enslaved for 400 years. Moses was born a slave. At the time of his birth, the Egyptian pharaoh had given orders that all male children of Jews be cast in the river in order to reduce the population of the Israelites.

Moses' mother hid him for a brief time and placed him in a little basket by the riverbank, where he was found by the pharaoh's daughter. Moses' sister Miriam, who had been hiding and had watched this discovery, came forward and volunteered his real mother as a nurse. Throughout Moses' youth, she was able to plant and keep alive in him the knowledge and tradition of the Hebrew faith.

Moses, whose name means "to draw out of water," was raised in the splendor of the royal palace and educated in the most advanced civilization of that time. He was given every possible advantage of training and knowledge in science, mathematics, government, military, psychology, the occult wisdoms, and the magic of the priesthood. He was educated to become an Egyptian leader. Act I represents this first period of Moses' life during which his intellect and reasoning were well-trained.

He removed himself from the first act by slaying an Egyptian, which broke the power over him of all that Egypt stood for, but which also forced him to flee, alone and afraid. He had learned the science of governing others, but hadn't yet learned to govern himself. He forced justice at a drastic expense to himself.

Moses retreated to the desert of Midian, which is Arab country. At a water well, he rescued seven sisters from the unwanted advances of some desert marauders; and he was invited to live with their family. He married one of the sisters and became a shepherd. It was an enormous change from living in royal splendor to becoming a wandering tribesman mingling with the common people. But this was an important part of his education, for he learned to understand them, to know what was in the hearts of the average people and what caused their unhappiness and suffering; and he gained an understanding of the human predicament he could have never learned in the palace. It balanced his academic with his practical training and also made him want to help. But more importantly, in the solitude of desert life, he learned to rule himself. His mind had been trained for leadership, but not his heart. Before Moses could become a great leader, it was necessary that he gain spiritual understanding. Tending sheep in Midian gave him ample time for the meditation, prayer, and quiet reflection that developed in him a meekness—not toward men, but toward God—a spiritual "teachableness" that gave priority to inspiration and intuition over the often overwhelming evidence of the outer senses. Then came the divine revelation of the "burning bush" (a symbol of something that occurred within him), an awesome vision of the eternal, unseen presence and power of the "living God" as the great reality in life. He dared answer, *"Here am I,"* (Exod. 3:4) ready to commit himself; still, there was much doubt. Doubt seems to be a strong, lingering influence in us. It seems to take so much evidence of the power of God to overcome it. Like all of us, Moses doubted his own capabilities; and he wanted to know more about the power and the nature of the Spirit that called him. God's answer to all his doubt was: . . . *I AM THAT I AM.* . . . (Exod. 3:14 A.V.) I am God, the only presence and power in the universe, the infinite possibilities of the all-embracing good, the only authority you need to accomplish anything good. I am the eternal God of all creation that indwells you as your help in every need.

I AM THAT I AM is said to have appeared on the walls of Egyptian temples. Moses possibly had seen the phrase many times, and he knew its significance. With this spiritual illumination, he realized then that the only possibility for liberation of mankind was through a recognition and a working faith in the great central Truth of the one, eternal, indwelling God. He then understood his own mission, which was to educate others to the divine way out of bondage and to demonstrate this liberation by leading the Israelites on a great symbolic Exodus through the "wilderness." It was his mission to lead his own people and thereby show all of us the way into a new life and introduce us to our everlasting choice: *Bondage or liberty, which?*

From then on, Moses' amazing resources came from his faith in the indwelling, living God. Nothing thwarted him or made him give up. When others saw trouble, lack, danger, he saw possibility and opportunity. Even when others saw "pillars of clouds" or "pillars of fire," he saw God. From that time on, Moses identified very closely with God. He was constantly alert to recognizing, accepting, and being grateful for "things not seen." He saw with the "eyes of faith," and acted from the power of Spirit. From then on he certainly needed all this, for was there ever anyone who had more to contend with than Moses?

There was the long cat-and-mouse game with the pharaoh to " . . . 'let my people go' . . . " (Exod. 5:1) representing a contest of might between God and the pharaoh. First, there were displays of magic, then a series of plagues in which the pharaoh would alternately consent and then withdraw his consent, until the last plague, the death of the firstborn, at which time (now known as the Passover) the Hebrews were able to escape.

Then there were the incredible events of the Red Sea, in which the pharaoh thought the Hebrews would be stopped.

A youngster once came home from his first Sunday school class at church and his father asked him to tell what he had learned. The boy said, "We learned about Moses crossing the Red Sea." The father said, "Tell me about it." The boy then said, "Moses was helping his people escape from Egypt and the pharaoh began to chase them in chariots. When the Hebrews got to the Red Sea, they built a pontoon bridge and crossed over. When the Egyptians began to cross the bridge, Moses got on his walkie-talkie, called in the artillery, and blew them up." His father said, "Did they tell you that?" The boy said, "Well, Dad, if you don't believe that, you would never believe what they did tell me."

The spiritual importance of the Red Sea story is that it was the site of one of our most encouraging biblical truths: . . . *"Fear not, stand firm, and see the salvation of the Lord, which he will work for you today . . . ."* (Exod. 14:13)

Then there was the wilderness itself. It was the

desert south of Canaan, lonely and dreary—a place in which it was very difficult to find food and water. Yet God constantly met their needs through Moses. Fresh manna was provided each day. Instructions were given to strike a rock with a rod and water would flow. Shoes never wore out. Clouds and pillars of fire guided them. But still they complained. They murmured that there wasn't enough food or water; the days were too hot, the nights too cool. They had become so accustomed to slavery that it had robbed them of their self-reliance and courage. After each need had been met, they quickly forgot. They whimpered and complained about their hard lot and their leader, and they remembered only the food and security of Egypt.

Because they complained, their future seemed dim, they lost their perspective about their past, and they saw everything in the present in a distorted way. Nothing was in focus; everything was wrong. Moses more than once had to put down a revolt, and he became a strict and sometimes a harsh leader. They had entered the desert free, but as an unorganized mob of slaves. It was only Moses who had been lastingly inspired—and it took him "forty years" of wandering in the desert to shape them into enough of a nation so that they could enter the Promised Land.

As they wandered, many problems arose, so

Moses established laws and trained other leaders to help him. The Ten Commandments were inspired through Moses to teach the people a way out of primitive bondage into a higher way of life. At the suggestion of his father-in-law Jethro, Moses organized people into groups and divisions with a chain of command and the delegation of responsibility and authority that are still used today in our courts, business, and military as principles of management and organization.

There was one early attempt to enter the Promised Land. Twelve scouts were sent into the land of the Philistines, where they found that the grapes were huge, but so were the Philistines. It made them feel like "grasshoppers," so all but two voted against it. Fear and forgetting what God had already done shut them out; and they had to complete the full cycle of forty years of wandering in order to let the old generation of former slaves die off before they could enter the Promised Land.

Finally the Hebrew nation, having become a new generation of desert-trained people, approached Canaan from the East. It was a touching and inspiring scene as old Moses finally saw Canaan. His eyes had "never dimmed," but he knew he could not enter. He had made one mistake. He had spoken the word "we," thereby taking credit when he had brought forth water with a rod. It hardly seems fair that after all he had done so well and faithfully he should have to pay so high a price for one mistake. (It doesn't, however, when we understand the inner meaning of it, which we will come to later.)

The mission of Moses, historically, was to lead the Israelites out of the bondage of Egypt into the Promised Land. Spiritually, it was to demonstrate the exodus possible for all people from a self-imprisoned bondage toward a life as lived by a son of God. How did Moses do it? Leadership. Moses was a deliverer, a conqueror, a lawgiver, a shepherd, a soldier, a diplomat, a writer, a teacher, a prophet; but overall, he was an executive—a leader!

Everything in the story of Moses has a remarkable parallel for us in our experience of growing in Truth. When we take our stand in the choice: *Bondage or liberty, which?* we have begun our spiritual exodus. Moses, the pharaoh, Egypt, the wilderness, and the Promised Land all represent components of this three-act drama that begins in us. Much of the inner significance is obvious. Everyone understands how easy it is to drift into binding habits, how difficult to quit a bad habit, how much more difficult to escape prejudices, fears, and reliance for security on the things of the world—money, position, and prestige. Sooner or later we all come to the conclusion that when we live with all our attention directed to outer effects, we are in bondage; then, by grace, a spiritual insight is born in us (as in Moses), capable of being raised up to lead all our thoughts and feelings out of their negative patterns. We first nurture and protect this newly-awakened awareness; then we begin to educate and train our intellects by studying the principles of Truth, especially the mental law of cause and effect.

It is a great step forward when we learn that our thinking produces our experience and that changing our thoughts begins to change effects so that we are no longer completely at the mercy of chance and circumstance. Then one day we "slay an Egyptian," a belief in bondage, and we are no longer secure in the land of bondage. This forces the issue; we have taken our stand and we must move out toward freedom. In act two, we learn to retreat into meditation, prayer, and quiet reflection. We become receptive ("teachable") to our inner spirit, and we grow in spiritual understanding (or as we say, "Build consciousness"). Then, the "burning bush" becomes the first real experience of true spiritual consciousness which leaves us with great awe, but still with doubts. Yet, we move on into the third act, actually beginning to rely on spiritual Truth as a source of inspiration, guidance, protection, and overcoming power.

And how graphic the symbols of the plagues are for the struggles we have in "breaking" the power of our egos—the ruling pharaoh of our sense consciousness. The Red Sea is race consciousness, the largest barrier, which we cross by learning to "stand fast" and really trust the power of Spirit. There is the continuing complaining and murmuring of our unspiritual multitudes of "thought people." How they nag us and keep us working! And sometimes we send out scouts—beautiful thoughts—to explore, but the giant obstacles make our "thought people" feel like grasshoppers. As we wander and train, the old enslaved concepts begin to die off, our spiritual thoughts increase, and one day we're ready to enter a new level of spiritualized consciousness—a new dimension of being.

There is a promised land—a fulfillment—for each stage of spiritual unfoldment. When we let the higher law of our being (the I AM) take over, we are led through many experiences for our training and growth. Our individual stages of growth and mastery are relative, yet ever unique. Therefore, the education and development of our personal inner leadership qualities and our need to follow the guidance of great spiritual Truth is continuous and progressive, yet always based on the same principles. How did Moses do it? The ultimate success of soul leadership is found in the first of the Ten Commandments: *"I am the Lord your God, . . . "* (Exod. 20:2) (whose nature is) *I*

AM THAT I AM. He worshiped the one God and trusted the one Presence and Power as his help in every need.

This brings us to the last thing. What was the inner meaning of Moses' one mistake? It involved his intellectual state of development and the "second bondage" it can cause. As we learn to work with the basically good and helpful laws of mental science (through the intelligent use of which our subconscious powers become capable of great accomplishment), we can begin to believe in our own mind action, with at least subtle pride, as a "personal" power. We begin to think that everything in life depends on our human consciousness; and this can become an awesome responsibility, for we get not only the credit but the blame. This belief, by the enactment of our own law, limits us considerably. We forget it is, "Not I, but the Father within that doeth the works." In an intriguing and memorable way this was incorporated into the story to show us that true freedom, growth, and mastery are always found in God's infinite intelligence, His divine power, and His omnipresent love. "Moses" in us needs to learn to go to God for every need. Our understanding use of law, which is our great guide and support, can lead us to the border of the promised land of spiritual consciousness; but it is spiritual power that carries us in.

The mission of Moses (in us) is ended—in each stage—when we have faithfully complied with all the spiritual law we understand and then let go and let God, resting in the realization that God adds the increase. God always has higher good in store for each of us if we are faithful to the law and stay open and receptive to *I AM THAT I AM*.

Jonah—A Mouthful

The story of Jonah has become one of the most familiar and at the same time the least understood of all Bible accounts—both for the same reason: the incredible fish story. When it was written, at another time, in another age, its real meaning was easily understood.

Now, the mention of Jonah or any fish story can bring a smile. It is well known that most fishermen catch their best fish by the "tale," and that there is a miracle of sorts involved in all fish stories—nothing grows quite so fast as a fish from the time it bites until it gets away!

The big news in the story of Jonah is that it is the man who gets away from the fish, and for many people that has been hard to swallow. Maybe we can get past the question of credibility with this story: A man said to a fisherman, "I notice that in telling about the fish you caught, you vary the size with different listeners." "Yes," answered the fisherman. "I never tell a man more than I think he'll believe."

Perhaps, if the author of Jonah had foreseen how much the allegory of the great fish was to distract us western Christians from his true message, he might have used a less confusing and more believable illustration. But the Old Testament wasn't witten with us in mind at all.

If we can get past the hard-to-swallow literal picture of a man inside a fish to what the writer was really trying to say in this parable, we shall find that the wonderful story is exceedingly valuable and inspiring as a practical spiritual lesson.

There really was a man named Jonah; and he actually lived in the northern kingdom of Israel about 750 B.C., when Jeroboam II was king of Israel. But, the story itself was written perhaps 300 years later, at a time when the Jewish people were facing a great national problem; and it was written to correct and guide them through and beyond their problems by revealing to them a higher vision of God and of their own mission as the "chosen of God."

Let's look at the story, which is in the form of a three-act play. Jonah was a "reluctant" prophet. That is, he could receive divine instructions and directions; but because of his narrow stern religious concepts, the instructions were beyond his level of spiritual understanding.

Jonah had been commissioned by God to leave his homeland and go to the people in Nineveh to share his Jewish belief in God so that they too could be saved. But he didn't like the people of Nineveh. Nineveh was the capital of Assyria, the despised nation that had sent his people into captivity; and it was also a nation whose glory and great wealth the Hebrews envied. Jonah didn't want the Ninevites to be saved. He wanted them to get everything he thought they had coming. So, when God instructed Jonah to go east, he got on a ship and *went west* as far as he could go! And that is what Tarshish, or Spain, meant to them: the end of the Earth. It was their way of saying, in story form, that Jonah did exactly the opposite of what God wanted him to do. He utterly disobeyed God.

So we read that once they were at sea, the Lord caused a great wind to come up which threatened the ship. The frightened sailors cast lots to see who was causing the storm. When it was determined that it was Jonah, he confessed his plight. He told the sailors he was a Hebrew and that he had disobeyed the Hebrew God and was now trying to escape God's presence. He told them to throw him overboard. They didn't really want to; but for the good of the others, they tossed him into the sea. Then the story says a *great fish* swallowed Jonah—and the curtain drops on the first act.

Jonah spent three days in the great fish; and, as the curtain rises on the second act, we are given a little of what you might call *inside* information.

Jonah, realizing that he couldn't get away from God, started to pray. The Jewish prayers were usually sung, repeated downright woefully in a sad, mournful, dissonant minor key. Now, it isn't in the Bible—and my Bible history teacher said he hadn't read it anywhere, but he had always suspected—that Jonah wasn't much of a singer. In fact, he said Jonah must have been a lousy singer because it wasn't long before the great fish just couldn't stand it any longer. It came up close to shore, opened its mouth in a great yawn, and "burp," up came Jonah, tossed right back where he had started.

And as the curtain drops on the second act, we have a sadder but wiser Jonah. Once again, Jonah was commissioned by God to go to Nineveh. He was given a second chance! From his first experience he had learned the hard way that he couldn't evade God's command. So this time he did part of what he was told—in letter, but not in spirit. It was meant to be a great mission of mercy, a ministry to warn the Ninevites so that they could change their ways. Though he was reluctant, he must have been some preacher. We read that when he was yet a day's journey from the city, he cried and said: *"Yet forty days and Nineveh shall be overthrown."* (Jonah 3:4) And they believed every word he said! That entire city, so huge that it took three days to walk around, was completely converted. What a revival!

Jonah should have been glad and grateful. But, although he had done what he was commanded, he was really counting on God's wrath to doom the people. And when they were given a second chance, he was extremely disappointed. In fact, he was angry, bitter, and personally wounded by the outcome. Jonah had no conception of Jesus' spiritual teaching: " . . . *Love your enemies and pray for those who persecute you.* . . . " (Matt. 5:44) He didn't understand that to be "chosen" of God doesn't mean to be privileged or favored, but to be a "light"—a guide, an example, and a spiritual servant to all others. So Jonah, instead of returning home, went to the outskirts of Nineveh, built a shelter out of sticks, and sat down to sulk.

As the story continues, it tells that as Jonah sat there, God caused a big plant (gourdvine) to grow up over his little booth overnight to shade him and give him a little comfort. But then God turned right around and prepared a worm to kill the plant just at the time it was most needed, during a hot east wind. Jonah, who had at first been hurt and angry when Nineveh hadn't been destroyed, was now just as hurt and angry because the plant had been destroyed. He became so fretful, irritable, and full of self-pity that he wanted to die.

Then, with good timing, God made His point. In effect, He said: "If you feel that sorry about a plant that died, which you had nothing to do with planting or caring for, how do you think I feel about thousands of my own children who had .

never had a chance to know right from wrong?"

And the curtain drops. The story ends quietly, but with the marvelous unveiling of God's great concern for all His children—not a selected few.

Now comes something really interesting. This story of Jonah matches very closely something that happened to the Jewish nation. It had figuratively been swallowed up by Babylonia and carried off into captivity. But shortly after that, the Persian Empire conquered Babylonia; and the new king, Cyrus the Great (he was called the "king of kings"), had allowed the Jews to return home, giving them a second chance to rebuild their temple and their beloved Jerusalem. The original homeland—"the Promised Land"—had, in the meantime, been overrun with pagans. To protect and strengthen the returning Jews in their heritage, Ezra, a scribe and religious leader, had established severe laws, intensifying Jewish exclusiveness. Marriage and fraternization with outsiders were prohibited; regulations were enacted and enforced on the most minute details of their lives, with a strong emphasis on the authority and dignity of the priesthood. This inevitably caused some reactions. (The book of Jonah, as well as the book of Ruth, was written by enlightened Hebrews as brave and noble protests against the narrow, intolerant attitude that the Hebrews had generally developed against those not of their own race and religion.) The author of Jonah had gained higher thoughts about God than his contemporaries; and these truths were woven into this wonderful drama—a story in which the nation is personified as one man, Jonah, the historical prophet out of the past. It is a written sermon in story form, a moving parable about the fatherhood of God to all people. Its message is the brotherhood of man. The author used literature and oral tradition that were familiar to practically everyone at the time it was written.

He drew from folklore the episode of the "great fish" which was found in many parts of the ancient world—Mesopotamia, India, and Egypt—and he added the anecdote of the rapidly growing vine to illustrate and provide a colorful background to the story. This story of a man swallowed by a fish is a dramatic, novel way to show the futility of disobeying God's command and also to provide a means within the story to bring Jonah back where he started. The gourdvine enabled the author to quickly develop the contrast between Jonah's narrow-minded unreasonableness and God's patience, mercy, and love for all people. And it shows also that God didn't condemn Jonah, but gave him time to reflect and judge himself.

The story vividly shows that Jonah, in his religious pride, had a very definite serious limit, but that God does not. And it isn't a somber story; it is meant to be entertaining. It has a thread of humor and fun that runs through it eastern-style, not only in the characteristics of Jonah and Nineveh, but in the characteristics of God, Himself. There is no mention of the author; but we know it was written in the time of Ezra because it describes Nineveh, which was later destroyed. Nineveh was probably the author's choice for the scene of the "preaching" because traditionally it was the most depraved and despised of all non-Jewish cities.

This is a great book. Its value as a spiritual message lies in its ideals, not its facts; and of course all the Jewish people for whom it was written understood what it meant. From their point of view, they acknowledged that they had disobeyed God and as a result they had been "swallowed up" by Babylon; then they were given another chance. What were they going to do with it? The book of Jonah gave them a solution. It pointed to a higher vision of God and a new outlook on life—the truth that God is God of the Gentiles as well as the Jews.

It can mean even more for us because it can now be seen that the story of Jonah is a high point in the Old Testament. Indeed, its spiritual value shows Judaism at its best.

Nowhere in pre-Christian literature can be found a broader, loftier, more tender conception of God. It is a mountainpeak in the Old Testament, from which can be seen the spiritual teaching of Jesus about a God of love.

When we get by the hard-to-swallow literal interpretation and understand it in terms of the original purpose and eastern style, we find that this little story really says a "mouthful"; it is a tremendous message with profound depth. The book of Jonah is a classic answer to prejudice and religious exclusiveness. But the true goal of this short but powerful lesson is a paramount way to think about God—to believe in God's loving-kindness and infinite care. Jonah is an appeal to lift our vision, widen our horizons, and strengthen our purposes to make a higher, more loving concept of God real and operative in our own lives.

One side of the lesson, of course, is to never let anyone between you and your highest belief in God. Don't let the theology or feelings of anyone else keep your God down to the size of his or her mind. Measure God by the mind that was in Jesus Christ, who knew God as a loving, forgiving, universal Father of all humanity.

The other side applies directly to each of us, personally and privately. Many people wonder why they don't get more out of life. Like Jonah, they set the limits and then get sulky. We each have a commission from God, something that needs to be accomplished through us. We each are designated by God to be a creative center of spiritual growth and progress. We are meant to be "about our Father's business" evolving from "glory to glory" God's indwelling nature into our own lives and worlds. It is our commission from God to let Christ be formed in us!

Is our idea of God growing? If you want more out of life, a second chance at anything, lift up your idea of God; and grow into it.

The Good Shepherd—Forever

One of the most memorable accounts in the Bible is based on the quiet, touching, recurrent drama of a shepherd caring for his sheep in the hills of Palestine. Perhaps there are no finer or more beautiful words in all literature to help us realize a spiritual intimacy with God and inspire us with a sense of eternal security than The 23d Psalm.

Certainly it is the pearl of all the Psalms and the most perfectly metrical poem in the Bible. The lyrical beauty of its words alone are a magical delight. It has been called "the simplest, sweetest song ever sung" (psalms were sung in biblical days). It has also been referred to as "a nightingale singing in the world's dark night of loneliness and need."

It has been memorized by generation after generation of Jews and Christians; and the familiar words of its winsome verse have brought a priceless message that reaches the depths of every needy heart, takes the sting out of any tragedy, and also can restore a delightful lilt to life.

This beautiful psalm is credited to King David, the greatest hero of the Old Testament. But in Hebrew Bible tradition, it might have been written for David, or about David, rather than by David.

Some biblical scholars feel it might have been written even as late as the return from the exile, hundreds of years after David, when the author had been able to come home again to the Promised Land after having suffered much in foreign captivity; and he is thanking God for all that God had done to bring his people through that grim ordeal.

The psalm is fascinatingly personal and intimate. It is not a petition; it asks for nothing. It is a realization, an affirmation, and an appreciation for God's unfailing care—a direct, intimate, and individual approach to a loving God, with the emphasis wholly on God's goodness, a relationship between man and God that didn't exist with most of the ancient concepts of a distant, aloof, wrathful diety.

Yet, in this ancient jewel, the author has unveiled the overwhelming sublime truth that the Lord God Almighty, who created all the universe and set the stars in their courses, and who transcends all time and space, has a personal, loving interest in each of us.

It doesn't seem to make too much difference who wrote the psalm if we know it is genuine—the author is speaking from ripe experience. He has really tried out the supporting power of God in some tough times and found that his Lord could always be trusted and relied upon as a very present help in every area and need of life. In this psalm, the poet has pulled back the curtain to the invisible side of creation and revealed a new vision of the comforting nearness of the spiritual presence of God and the intimate, loving, caring relationship of God to each of us individually that a shepherd has to his sheep.

The Lord is my shepherd—this sets the theme for the whole relationship. In Bible lands, the shepherd was the local hero. The word "shepherd" came to mean "friend, companion, guide." A shepherd was also equipped to protect and supply, combining authority with care, often suggesting a relationship that was parental, even angelic. In the olden days in Palestine, therefore, a shepherd became a marvelous symbol for God, picturing a living Presence with us every moment, loving, guiding, fulfilling each of us as though we were the only one.

Hospital nurses sometimes write the letters "T.L.C." on the bed chart of a sick child, meaning "tender loving care." The 23d Psalm is the "T.L.C." psalm of God's "Tender Loving Care" for each of His children. And what a profound difference it makes to be able to dissolve the barriers of separation and use the word "my" in relation to God. Then it is no longer theory or theological abstraction but a heartfelt union that lifts, comforts, and blesses. He knows each one intimately. The Psalmist dared call the eternal cosmic God his shepherd; and we each can know that God is that to us: kind, benevolent, devoted to our ultimate welfare, never driving, forcing, threatening, or under any circumstance deserting us or damning us, but leading us, as a shepherd, ever toward our highest good—asking only that we follow Him step by step.

Hundreds of years after the writing of The 23d Psalm, Jesus took up this supremely beautiful indentification as divine shepherd by declaring: *"I am the good shepherd . . . ."* (John 10:14) The 23d Psalm was fulfilled in the person of Jesus the Christ. Jesus came to reveal Christ. It was from the Christ within Himself that Jesus was speaking when He said: *"I am the good shepherd . . . ."* Jesus' use of the words "I am" corresponds to God's use of the "I AM" in Exodus as a name for His spiritual Presence indwelling man which Jesus manifested in the fullness of Christhood. Christ is the spiritual self, the God-Image individualized in all people.

Christ in us, God's indwelling Spirit, likewise proclaims: "I am the good shepherd—I have always been with you—always, even through sickness, trouble, lack—waiting, helping when I could." We need to identify Christ in us with Jesus, the good and perfect Shepherd.

With this understanding, we can affirm: *The Lord is my shepherd, I shall not want.* This doesn't mean that we will never suffer material deprivation. We are required to recognize a deeper truth than that. Our great need is for God Himself—for the realization of His invisible, spiritual essence and qualities from which all our supply is made manifest. God constantly gives of Himself. He is in all His gifts. The crowning gift of God is Christ, His potential nature in us; for in Christ there is the fullness of God. This Good Shepherd that dwells in each of us can supply every need, satisfy every desire, accomplish every plan and purpose God has for us. In truth, the Good Shepherd is not the supplier, He is the very supply itself.

We need to commit ourselves to the way of the indwelling Christ. We need faith to hold steadfast to the spiritual Truth that the presence of God in us is our own inner supply at hand. We need to believe that God, the Father in us, cares and is ever desiring to give of His good plans and kingdom, an abundance of all things we rightly need and desire. Prosperity is not a condition in our outer affairs, it is a state of consciousness. Sheep don't ask for miracles from the shepherd; there is no need for this, for they simply trust Him from day to day. We need to trust the indwelling Good Shepherd to daily bring forth that which is for our highest good in the form of ideas, Truth, substance, and love that blesses, heals, and prospers us in our spiritual growth. Our needs are met through the riches of consciousness.

Charles L. Allen in "God's Psychiatry," tells this story:

Immediately after World War II, the allied armies gathered up many hungry, homeless children and placed them in large camps. They were abundantly fed and cared for. However, at night none of them could sleep well. They seemed restless and afraid. Finally a psychologist thought of a solution. After the children were put to bed, they were each given a slice of bread to hold. If they wanted more to eat, that was provided. But this particular slice of bread was not to eat—just to hold. It produced marvelous results. The child would go to sleep unconsciously feeling that he would have something to eat tomorrow. That assurance gave him a calm and peaceful rest. The 23d Psalm can give us something of the same feeling—*The Lord is my shepherd, I shall not want*—we need only hold to one Truth that God in the midst of us is our abounding supply and that this eternal Shepherd has made abundant plans for tomorrow and forever. This is the only sense of security that lasts.

. . . *he makes me lie down in green pastures. He leads me beside still waters; he restores my soul. He leads me in paths of righteousness for His name's sake.*

Life is often anything but green pastures and still waters. Most of the time we live in a world of freeways, red tape, and constant problems, strife, and disrupting events. And if we forget, we have the press, radio, and TV to constantly remind us of the "bad news." It is, therefore, more necessary than ever for us to learn what it means that God restores our souls.

Through food and sleep, He restores daily our minds and bodies. Soul restoration comes when we cultivate an inner life that opens us to the lavish green pastures and still places of consciousness—at the center of our being—from which come peace, faith, joy, love, new strength, and life more abundant. . . . *he restores my soul;* this is a direct and clear affirmation, related to prayer and meditation, that God is an inexhaustible spiritual reservoir, forever restoring, strengthening, and rebuilding our souls from within.

When you faithfully practice daily prayer and meditation, you will begin to experience marvelous, peaceful, restful states of consciousness. That peace, which is . . . *the peace of God, which passes all understanding* . . . (Phil. 4:7) is the platform for all creativity. And from this clear, peaceful awareness you begin to see yourself being led and guided.

He leads me in paths of righteousness . . . . This does not mean moral correctness. Jesus made quite a point of telling us that dealing with outer effects is placing the cart before the horse, whitewashing the outside and letting the inside remain a mess. *Paths of righteousness* is what happens in prayer, producing the right direction in consciousness, the right attitudes. He especially guides us in the paths of right thought, leading us through all the dangers and temptations toward a spiritual goal—according to a divine blueprint.

Then we come to a beautiful promise: . . . *for his name's sake,* meaning that whatever God does is always a reflection of Himself, always true to His character. God can never send anything less than His perfect, hallowed nature.

Even though I walk through the valley of the shadow of death, I fear no evil; for thou art with me; thy rod and thy staff, they comfort me. The Psalmist now extends the affirmation that God's life and love never fail us—to include even the experience of death. What we humanly call death has no real permanence or diminishment but is merely a doorway we all pass through to the next phase of existence. Death is a necessary and beneficial transition to larger life. It is a release, a new start, the beginning of a new life. The shadow of death is the fear of it. When we have overcome the fear of death, we will have dissolved the last enemy that bars us from a joyous sense of eternal security that knows no bounds.

The "shadow of death" literally meant "deep shadow," which can include all the dark, undesirable experiences and seeming losses in life we call evil. Even in the shadows of death or life, God can be trusted. For in His plan, they too can contain purpose—hidden lessons and messages that help us grow. Out of anything that to human sight seems to be entirely dark and evil can rise the all-victorious Spirit of God in us; therefore, there is ultimately nothing to fear. One of the greatest lessons that can be learned in the spiritual life is that in Spirit and Truth there is nothing to fear.

. . . *thy rod and thy staff* . . . are symbols of the most truth-worthy guides and supports we have in life—the unfailing laws of principles of God.

Thou preparest a table before me in the presence of my enemies; thou anointest my head with oil, my cup overflows. In the East there was a tradition we don't know much about, but should, in which people invited their enemies to lavish banquets. They entertained them much more generously than they did their friends, for they felt that their friends were already friends. It was an attempt at reconciliation. Here, God Himself becomes the conciliatory host, sitting us down with our invisible enemies and arranging and providing the spiritual means of forgiveness and release from our resentments, fears, and animosities.

. . . *thou anointest my head with oil* . . . meant special consecration for a new task. The word *Christ* meant "the anointed." God is constantly honoring and consecrating us to further and greater divine service as His spiritual image and likeness.

. . . *my cup overflows.* Any realization of the presence of God is a joyous occasion. Such an experience leaves us bubbling over with estatic appreciation for all the gifts, qualities, and graces we receive from God.

Surely goodness and mercy shall follow me all the days of my life; and I shall dwell in the house of the Lord for ever. Do you believe in angels? Consider "goodness" and "mercy" as two of your personal "guardian angels," two of the Good Shepherd's steadfast attributes constantly in action, never forsaking, never deserting, guaranteeing eternal, loving security.

The . . . *house of the Lord* . . . is a state of consciousness that is aware of the presence of God. It is built on the recognition that we live, move, and have our being in God, and that wherever we are, God is. His Spirit becomes increasingly active in us by our becoming aware of it and letting it find expression through us. Practice His presence by knowing: *He is with me now; He is guiding every step of my life; He is leading me victoriously through all the experience in my life;* and

more and more you will remain in that consciousness and in the secure awareness that His abiding
presence is your eternal home. The 23d Psalm is a
song of praise, joy, thanksgiving, and trust to the
ever-present loving God that lives in each of us. It
speaks to all of us. It reaches every heart that is
open. But we must learn to trust the Good Shepherd. It takes practice, persistence, diligent attention to learn to "still" the human and from the "still
waters" let God manifest in us as the Good Shepherd.

An actor once spent a good deal of time practicing a reading of The 23d Psalm. Even with his
extensive training in elocution, however, he
wasn't satisfied. He asked an elderly minister to
read it and as he did, it brought tears to the actor's
eyes. When the minister had finished, he said: "I
understand now. I know the words, but you know
the Shepherd."

But, of course, the words of The 23d Psalm are
still priceless as a way to get to know the Shepherd. These words have been breaking in on the
hearts of people for thousands of years, inspiring,
leading, giving courage, comfort, strength, and
spiritual assurance. Hearing the words has quickened countless heavy hearts with trust and joy.
Let these same words work and become flesh in
you until you know that Good Shepherd who
lives in you—forever.

75

The Christmas of Your Life

The Christmas anthology is probably the greatest gathering of traditions, customs, and stories of any event in human history. It draws together thousands of years of history and harmoniously integrates the customs, the folklore, the hopes, the longings, the spiritual aspirations, and the religious beliefs of many people from many nations. It is the one thing so far that has truly brought the East and the West together.

When you think about it, much of the Christmas story and its traditions are make-believe. It started with the factual birth of Jesus Christ; but, along with this nativity story, we now find a charming blend of Santa Claus, Christmas trees, mistletoe, candy canes, Yule logs, Scrooge, and even "Rudolph the Red-Nosed Reindeer." They are almost as much a part of Christmas as the original story; and, even if none of it were an actual fact, all of it is true spiritually. It is a story that truly belongs to all humankind. The greatest dimension is reached when we realize that Christmas is really our story—the drama of the birth of Christ in us.

I would like, therefore, to reach back through the anthology into the Bible, to focus on the essentials and bring them together so that we each can experience the Christmas of our lives. We usually think of the Christmas story as beginning with the story of the birth of Jesus, but actually it began in the Bible approximately 600 years before His birth, with the prophecy of Isaiah: *For to us a child is born, to us a son is given; and the government will be upon his shoulder, and his name will be called "Wonderful Counselor, Mighty God, Everlasting Father, Prince of Peace." Of the increase of his government and of peace there will be no end. . . .* (Isa. 9:6)

The only description we have then about the actual birth of Jesus are the few lines found in two of the Gospels—Matthew and Luke. These Gospel stories were written down long enough after the life of Jesus, perhaps thirty years, so that each is different. The book of Matthew was written mainly to the Jews to convince them that Jesus, whom they had rejected, had actually been their long-awaited Messiah. It was framed in references to their promised Davidic Messiah, the King of the Jews, connected with important Jewish personages from the past and with the grandeur of palaces and kings and priests. It reminded the Jews that even Wise Men outside of Jerusalem and the Jewish religion had recognized Jesus as the Messiah and had traveled far distances to honor His birth.

The Gospel of Mark was written mostly for the Romans. A Roman wouldn't have been the least bit interested in the birth of a Jewish baby or impressed by that kind of promise of power and glory, so it was never mentioned.

Luke gives an entirely different glimpse of the story of Jesus. Luke was a gentile, a gentle Hellenistic Greek physician. He was a humanist. He thought of the little things. He talked about the humble setting of a manger and shepherds and animals. And then he talked about an angel: *And in that region there were shepherds out in the field, keeping watch over their flock by night. And an angel of the Lord appeared to them, and the glory of the Lord shone around them, and they were filled with fear.* (Luke 2:8, 9)

Then, Luke took the story into a wonderful dimension. Matthew had traced the genealogy of Jesus back to Abraham to show that all Jews were related to this Messiah. Luke took the genealogy straight back to Adam and Eve, showing that Jesus was related to everyone. Luke took the story out of the exclusiveness of one people or one religion and gave it a worldwide setting with a universal meaning. *"Be not afraid; for behold, I bring you good news of a great joy which will come to all people; for to you is born this day in the city of David a Savior, who is Christ the Lord. And this will be a sign for you: you will find a babe wrapped in swaddling cloths and lying in a manger."* And suddenly there was with the angel *a multitude of the heavenly host praising God and saying, "Glory to God in the highest, and on earth peace among men with whom he is pleased!"* (Luke 2:10-14)

The book of John, so unlike the other three that it is not considered a synoptic gospel, is truly a metaphysical (spiritual) book; and it gives us the third great meaning of the Christmas story—the real meaning, the fullest meaning, the meaning that our well-intentioned religious leaders have diverted from us with astounding success throughout the ages—*the mystery hidden for ages.* (Col. 1:26)

We all tend to believe of course that Christ was born in a manger 2,000 years ago in Bethlehem. But actually, we read about the original birth of Christ in Genesis: *So God created man in his own image, in the image of God created he him; male and female he created them.* (Gen. 1:27) The image of God—the spirit of God in us—is Christ. Jesus Christ lived it out completely. But Christ is in every person. Jesus Himself said that. He once said: " . . . *before Abraham was, I am."* (John 8:58) That doesn't sound grammatically correct, but it is. Before Abraham was I AM. I AM is the name of the universal God, the Spirit of God in all men that Jesus represented. I AM, the ancient name of Christ—*the true light that enlightens every man was coming into the world* (John

1:9)—the spiritual image and likeness in which we were all created, our own true Self or, as the Apostle Paul said: *". . . Christ in you, the hope of glory."* (Col. 1:27)

So, in the account of Matthew, we have the historical setting of Jesus, born Christ 2,000 years ago. In Luke, we have the universal idea in which Jesus Christ became the central personage of our evolution Christward. Jesus, the Way-Shower, the Guide, the Elder Brother, the Example, the Savior of all mankind.

Once Jesus said: *"Truly, truly, I say to you, he who believes in me will also do the works that I do; and greater works than these will he do, because I go to the Father."* (John 14:12) The greatest tribute we can pay to Jesus is to acknowledge the Christ Spirit in ourselves. His mission was to introduce each of us to God's indwelling Spirit, the Father within each of us.

It is the book of John that gives us this third, individual meaning, that Christ lives in us, personally; and this book brings the Christmas story right into our own lives, right into the manger of our hearts. This means that you and every man, woman, and child who has ever been born and is alive right now is essentially the Christ in potential, a spiritual being with the seed of God at the core of his or her being. This means that, as God's child, Isaiah's promise and Jesus' great life apply to you. It is about you. Therefore, the Christmas story is really your story. And as it has been said: *Though Christ a thousand times in Bethlehem be born, if He is not born in thee, thy soul is still forlorn.*

The message will never be fulfilled until you understand that. All the ideas of the Christmas story have individual applications in you right now. All the main characters of the Bible story are involved in your own inner life in the Christmas that is to happen to you. Christmas has the power, the spiritual power, to quicken these deep things of Christ in you. To make the promise happen—to bring forth in you the great drama of Christmas—the real celebration of Christmas is always an inner experience that occurs in you in which Christ is born in your consciousness.

It all happens in consciousness; it is an inner drama in which spiritual awareness is quickened in you. The Christ Spirit is literally born into your awareness and becomes a vital part of your humanity. And the inn, the manger, Mary and Joseph, the Wise Men, Herod, the shepherds, the animals, and the great Star all have their role in the drama of your inner Christmas.

Let's start with the inn. The inn represents your intellect. There was no room in the inn. The baby was born, therefore, in the manger. The manger is your heart, your emotions. It doesn't make any difference what the condition of your heart is—it can be a stable—yet Christ can still be born.

We are again involved with our own thoughts and feelings in the part Joseph and Mary play in the Christmas drama.

Joseph was the human father of Jesus. Men in the Bible represent the intellectual part of your mind—your thinking ability. Joseph had an intellectual use that was very high. Yet, from the very beginning he really didn't understand the whole process. He was told that he wasn't even involved in the original conception of this spiritual birth. But he still consented and was very happy to be the human father of the child—to protect, guide, support, and become the important father role in helping to raise the child. Our intellect can do that. The right state of mind is very important to the growth of a new spiritual awareness in us.

Mary, as do all women in the Bible, represents the activity of our own emotional nature. Mary, the mother of Jesus represents the very highest emotional experience that human beings can have: pure intuition. And this is how the Christ Spirit comes to us: through intuition. We read that when Mary was inspired with the knowledge that she was to give birth to the Christ child, she kept these things secret and pondered them in her heart; and then she magnified the Lord.

It was through Mary that Jesus was born. It is

through the virgin awareness of pure intuition that the perfect Christ idea of our own spiritual identity is inspired. A pure heart always magnifies the Spirit of God in us.

Herod is also a part of our intellect, a very important part to know about. He is the puppet king, the human ego. Our ego is almost always threatened by the birth of something new, so threatened that it tries to kill out the idea. The only thing that ever really keeps us from growing is our own ego. This is what we need to get out of the way. We are not essentially human egos. Our ego identities are made up of all sorts of separate, diversified, and often conflicting concepts that we have stored in our memories along the way, coming together in many different ways and forming through us traits of thought and feeling that we call personality. We actually have many personalities within our human egos, but underneath is always the central identity of our true spiritual nature with all the possibilities represented in the birth of the Christ child in us.

The shepherds and sheep from the peaceful Judean countryside again introduce us to the inner scene of our intellectual and emotional processes. The shepherd is the humble, trustworthy, often simple type of thought that (like Joseph) watches and tends with loving care the flock of feelings that are under its charge. The shepherd is often the hero in the Bible, and we can establish this quality of kind and peaceful but strong leadership in our own intellect. We can use our minds to gently guide and take care of our little thoughts and chase after the black sheep, to transmute all things in us so that they truly follow the Christ. When we let the shepherd-type thought take charge of our emotions, then we are open to the angelic inspiration that can come.

Angels represent messages from God, divine inspiration and guidance that bring " . . . *good news of a great joy. . . .* " (Luke 2:10) The message of the ages is about . . . *Christ in you, the hope of glory.* (Col. 1:27) This is the good news that the heavenly multitudes sing about to each of us.

And then we come to the three Wise Men—*the three kings.* The Bible account doesn't mention the word *kings,* nor does it say how many there were, just . . . *wise men from the East* . . . . (Matt. 2:1) They were really Magi, astronomers and mystics. In the Bible, *East* symbolically means: *toward the rising sun; in the direction of the source, the spiritual realm of consciousness.* In the West, we are far more impressed by kings than by enlightened holy men. We also have a need for facts and statistics. It is very important for us to know who and how many. So, from the mentioning of three gifts, we have concluded that there were three kings; and in the Middle Ages, we even invented names for them. The Easterner, however, knew the poetry of the story and would no more strip it of its deeper meaning with facts than a wonder-filled child would try to figure out the aerodynamics of Santa's sleigh. Spiritually discerned, the Wise Men represent something wonderful in us. They represent that kind of higher wisdom and spiritual insight that can come right into our ordinary thoughts and feelings when we are open to the guidance of the great Star.

Charles Fillmore said that in the Bible a star always represents the possibilities of our own Christhood. Stars may seem very remote, but they are bright if we look up to them. The Wise Men saw the Star in the East. There are various Western speculations about the Christmas Star. It has been suggested that it was a nova, or an exploding star, or a conjunction of planets. But, as we often do, unless we are spiritually inclined, we overlook something. Very few people saw that Star. Herod didn't see it. Only the illumined saw that Star. That Star represents our higher aspirations, something that we can see only when we have the consciousness, the open spiritual receptivity of the Eastern Wise Men.

The Wise Men were led by inspiration to the birthplace of the Christ child, where they honored the Child with gifts and celebrated His birth. *Magi* comes from a word that has the same root as magnet and magic. Magnet: to draw to. Magic: to experience wonderment and excitement of things not understood. This is the special kind of consciousness that makes Christmas so special. To develop it, to be able to *see* that Star, we need to go apart awhile and experience the communion in the silence of the Secret Place. Here we can travel "East" into spiritual consciousness.

To be able to see that Star and follow it will bring forth the beautiful spiritual qualities of our true nature. These can be our gifts to the Christ child in us.

The Christ is the greatest gift of all, for it is the gift of God's own nature expressing in us as us. But the law for receiving is giving. This Christmas, for the Christmas of your life, give the gifts of the Wise Men to the Christ child in you. There are three gifts—gold, frankincense, and myrrh.

Gold represents the material possessions which, when properly regarded, are good and necessary mediums through which we work out the divine plan in our lives. They are temporal but can be given spiritual significance and used for the glory of God. Our gift to the Christ child is to dedicate it all to God. Dedicate everything you possess, tangible and intangible, to God, and everything in your life will become a force for good and a powerful magnet for everything you truly need in your process of growth.

Frankincense is an incense, a beautiful symbol of prayer that we send upward into higher consciousness toward our aspirations. We can surround ourselves during the Christmas season with an atmosphere of prayer, and this deep prayer commitment can open us to all sorts of wonderful things. Make even the activities of Christmas (like trimming the tree, sending cards, visiting friends, and buying and opening presents) prayerful experiences. This is prayer without ceasing, a great gift to the Christ child.

The last gift is myrrh, which seems a rather strange gift because it is embalming ointment. Myrrh is connected with burying the dead, with letting go of that which is no longer needed, especially those things that have a restricting or negating influence on us. (Paul said that by dying to these things daily, we begin our lives new each day.) It can also mean that not all the blessings in our lives appear as happy things. Many of the conditions that cause us to grow the most come to us in the form of adversities. Things that cause us to mourn can be converted by God into blessed experiences. If you have a heavy heart, an illness, a difficult problem, bring these to the Christ child as gifts. Turn your burdens over to the Christ Spirit, release them, and they will be transmuted and exchanged for new life.

So, these are the three gifts we give Christ for Christmas: a dedication to God of everything in our lives, a deep prayer commitment, and a trusting surrender of the lesser in our lives for the greater—a higher consciousness.

Perhaps the last thing to do, then, is to remember that Jesus Christ grew up into the most magnificent personage the world has ever known. He lived out the great message of *Christ in you, the hope of glory*. He was the Christ of God in every way, for only a Christ could reveal the Christ. He grew from an infant into a Godlike man and took the responsibility of the entire world on His shoulders. Friend, the Christ that can be born in you can do that for you. The Spirit of Christ can take over the government of the entire world and work out all the problems for the greatest good of all. But to do that Christ must first be born in you.

May Christmas happen to you this year as never before! May you be guided to that potentiality of Spirit that is waiting to be born in you! May you know that the prophecy of Isaiah is about Christ in you! May this be the Christmas of your life!

Jesus—The Master Teacher

We now shift gears from the Old Testament to the New Testament, and to Jesus Christ, the central figure and Master of masters in all life. Incredible as it may seem, and as important as Jesus is in Christianity, very little of it is based on what He Himself taught. Instead, His teaching has been relegated to an insignificant role, whereas ecclesiastical doctrines and dogmas of the theologians, which evolved through the centuries, have prevailed and predominated. The most important factor overlooked in Christianity is Jesus as a master teacher.

If you remember the book "Goodbye Mr. Chips" or the movie "Good Morning, Miss Dove," you will be reminded of the very special place a teacher can have in people's hearts. A most wonderful way to draw near to Jesus, as well as to learn and grow from what He taught, is to become a dedicated student of the Master. This is the relationship the original disciples shared with Jesus—teacher and student.

Jesus was a master teacher—a rabbi—highly respected even among his non-followers. For example, when Nicodemus, a ruler of the Jews, first came to Him, he addressed Jesus: *"Rabbi, we know that you are a teacher come from*

God. . . . " (John 3:2) Jesus was the greatest teacher ever. Yet, to this day, only relatively few people clearly understand what He meant.

There are two key words to remember in anything concerning His message. The key to understanding all His teachings is found in the words *spirit* and *truth*. Only a few things really mattered to Jesus. He concentrated all His effort on one objective: to induce all people to base all life on God (to *"worship in spirit and truth"* John 4:24). The two essentials of His message were the proclamation of the *kingdom* and the promise of *rebirth*.

The *kingdom* is a term brought forward from the ancient Hebrew attitude about *kingship* evolving from the ancient relationship with a human king. It pointed toward the sovereignty of God. Jesus brought a whole new interpretation, with the great emphasis on giving everyone a spiritual orientation to life. Jesus revealed that God's whole nature can only be known that way. To Jesus, all questions are answered by referring to the spiritual Truth about God. Everything in His teaching refers to the spiritual principles, laws, attributes, and power that govern and run the universe. And with His glowing revelation that God is the all-Good, loving, benevolent, heavenly Father of all humankind, spiritual Truth becomes a triumphant and radiant thing.

The belief that God is love has not been an obvious truth. As were the people of Jesus' day, we are often uncertain about God. Like Thomas, we need to be convinced. And we need to bear this in mind or we may miss a great deal of what Jesus taught.

The first thing Jesus had to do as a teacher was to inspire people to rethink and rediscover God on a much higher level. He placed before us an image of God that is entirely spiritual but with a joyous emphasis on loving God who is interested in flowers and birds and grass and yet, even more, knows and cares and can work through us to bring all things right in everything that concerns us.

A spiritual understanding of Jesus makes it easy to believe in a God of goodness and love. He believed in and constantly used the power and attributes of God; but He was most conscious and appreciated the nearness of God as the loving Presence He called *"Our Father,"* or *"the Father who dwells in me and does his works. . . . "* If there is a persistent difficulty in spiritually understanding what Jesus taught, it is, in part, replacing the old concept of God "out there" (steeped in notions of fear and punishment) with Jesus' concepts of a loving God abiding right within us. This was the one precious thing (the treasure hid in a field—the pearl of great price), the transforming, spiritual message about the inner kingdom. Everything in the gospel refers to the inner quickening, the inner growth, and the inner spiritual evolution by which we are lifted into new higher levels from God's spirit within us.

Jesus' term *rebirth* refers to new beginnings and spiritual breakthroughs into higher dimensions of life that are possible because of the transforming power of the spirit of God that indwells us. Jesus' teachings focus on the knowledge of the abundant spiritual life that expands and comes forth from the latent spirit qualities and forces of God in us. Jesus tells us how to live—always from the center to the circumference. He did not give us rules and ethics for our outer conduct; He taught us what we must observe within ourselves—the inner training and discipleships of our thoughts and feelings, with a "single eye" to the positive and good. Jesus gave us a blueprint for higher living based solely on Truth principles and spiritual possibilities. Again and again He emphasized that life proceeds from the heart and that a well-cared-for inner life produces a good outer life.

His good news was that we all possess this power when we let God rule our minds and hearts. Jesus holds up the magnificent ideal of each of us expressing our own God-given latent divinity. He taught us the eternal solution for every conceivable human problem by constantly directing us within to our own indwelling Christ Spirit. He told us to always seek his kingdom,

"... and all these things shall be yours as well." (Matt. 6:33) As an example, He established the universal kingdom of God in miniature in His own life. He was the Word—the explanation and expression of all God can be in a child of God.

Jesus taught the Truth He stood for, and He proved the Truth He taught. He was the greatest example in history of creative, spiritual living; and He said: *"Truly, truly, I say to you, he who believes in me will also do the works that I do; and greater works than these will he do. ..."* (John 14:12)

Jesus did not come to establish a new system of religious hierarchy based on rites, ceremonies, and outer observance. When we realize that Jesus was establishing His kingdom on the indwelling Spirit of God in each person, we will understand the difficulty of what He was doing in reintroducing people to God in a new way—in spirit and truth, and within themselves.

Mankind's interest is largely elsewhere—anywhere but within himself. Jesus' teachings, therefore, were established like the kingdom of heaven itself—in seeds and with the leavening power of Spirit. As a master teacher, Jesus knew as no one else that the way to teach is to draw forth from within and unfold the potential.

William Ellery Channing has written: *The great end in religious instruction is not to stamp our minds irresistibly on the young, but to stir up their own; not to make them see with our eyes, but to look inquiringly and steadily with their own; not to burden the memory, but to quicken and strengthen the power of thought.* This matches the correct definition of education which is *to draw forth.*

Jesus insisted that all of us have a latent aptitude for God's Truth. In His teachings He corrected our wrong views. He pointed out the great principles and law that can lead us in the right direction. He always appealed to the best in us. He sought to arouse and stimulate a spiritual hunger and thirst for God that would transform us from the depth of our beings. His teachings were directed to our deepest feelings and our highest aspirations. He sought always to open our minds and hearts to the divine influence that can truly remake us and the world around us and establish the kingdom of heaven on Earth.

Jesus planted the seeds of His teaching mostly in parables so that they would live and grow in our minds and hearts. Yet, in everything that Jesus did, as well as what He said, He was teaching some lesson, revealing something about the kingdom and spiritual rebirth. He taught lessons not to be forgotten—some realistic, some imaginative, some mysterious—all eternally true, yet totally applicable to us today. Jesus could also be very practical and a good psychologist with sound mental and emotional understanding. He revealed profound insights into the nature of our thinking, the way we get into trouble from wrong thinking, and how we can get out of it by changing our thoughts.

Jesus had no illusions about the human condition. He knew the weak spots and the wasted lives, and He never tried to explain away "sin" or "evil." He saw much of both, but He knew and taught that God could forgive any sin; and His teachings were not a list of *thou shall nots*. They were positive instructions for correct thinking and living from within.

His means of reaching people were varied. Sometimes He taught in the local synagogues or the Temple in Jerusalem. But He also taught anywhere and everywhere He could. We find Him teaching in the open country, the mountainside, from boats, in the desert, in the homes of friends, at a well in Samaria, even before Herod, and on the Cross. Whatever the case at hand, whether it was one person present or a huge crowd, He always used the opportunity to teach about the *"way,"* the *"truth,"* and the *"life."*

Jesus often told stories, but He rarely "preached." His language was classic, poetic, immortal, great, but simple. To all people of all ages and of every level of life, His teachings were understandable. Sometimes it was only a few words or just a hint. He sometimes acted out His lessons, especially in the miracles and the triumphal entry. He usually enriched His stories with intriguing characters to make them memorable, as in the stories of the prodigal son, the Good Samaritan, and the Pharisee and the publican. He lightened His lessons with Eastern-style fun and humor, and ridiculous exaggerations like swallowing a camel; perhaps there would be just a smile or a look. We have to remember the great magnetism that flowed from this Man of God; even His enemies always knew they were dealing with someone great.

Many things have to be "felt" in His teachings. In Matthew we read: . . . *the crowds were astonished at his teaching, for he taught them as one who had authority, and not as their scribes.* (Matt. 7:28) There is a truthfulness, a vital power and radiant energy that can be clearly felt 2,000 years later. In His teachings as in His life, Jesus had authority; but He was never authoritarian.

From His greatest parable, "The Prodigal Son," we learn from Jesus the great mystery and the practical lesson of why things can be as they are. The Father doesn't control the son. He leaves the son free to work out his own life and make his own choices. But when the son seeks and asks for the Father's help, the Father is always ready and waiting and responsive with that which is always in the son's highest good.

The hallmark of any great teacher is to enable his students to unfold their own potential. Jesus was for many reasons the greatest teacher who ever lived. But behind every word and act, behind His genius and magnificent personality is the highest Truth—for Jesus always represents Christ—

. . . *Christ in you, the hope of glory.* (Col. 1:27)

I once read this tribute to teachers: *To a child thrust into a strange world, a teacher is the best thing that can happen.* One teacher who is especially memorable to me, perhaps because what I was learning was rather precarious, was my first instructor in pilot training. He became so important to me that, when I finally soloed, it was as if he were there—still a guide and an inspiration.

We have all been thrust into a strange world, and we each have a great deal to learn—that's why we're here. We each have the greatest Teacher in the world if we want Him—Jesus, the Master Teacher. Avail yourself of this marvelous opportunity. Become His ardent student, His disciple; get vitally interested in what He taught.

Especially in the coming lessons about the teachings of Jesus, I invite you to learn from Him, to rethink things in your life about your personality, home, job, your values, purposes, and goals, and especially your resources. Learn to rethink everything in terms of what Jesus Christ really taught. Remember, Jesus said: " . . . *Lo, I am with you always. . . .* " (Matt. 28:20) You can have constantly with you the best Teacher who ever lived—Jesus Christ.

The Wondrous World Within

Jesus had one central theme in everything He taught—the kingdom of God. Yet never once did He literally define this kingdom. All His explanations and discourses about the kingdom were figurative, poetic, illustrative, or visionary. This was because Jesus' kingdom is not of this literal or three-dimensional world. It is a spiritual kingdom. His mission was to reveal to humankind the marvelous realm of Spirit and its ways and qualities.

So to plant the seed of a new concept, there are several general ways in which Jesus presented and emphasized His kingdom teaching. First, there are precepts—short, unadorned statements of Truth, special instructions for us, keys and clues to understanding and finding the kingdom. These often take the form of an invitation or promise. Jesus made wide use of precepts in presenting His Sermon on the Mount as a series of steps by which we approach the kingdom. These concise but still rather vague statements by Jesus are found throughout the four gospels. The important thing to remember about them is that they are all connected with Jesus' message of a spiritual kingdom.

Jesus also used the activities and events in His own life—at times His miracles—to present the kingdom to humankind. His entire life was a series of lessons to explain the spiritual kingdom to all people. Jesus also made extensive use of parables to teach and illustrate different aspects about the kingdom. Nearly all His parables begin, *"The kingdom is like . . . ,"* and then He gives a comparative story to illustrate.

Let's explore a little of the historical background of the heritage we all share in our present concepts about the kingdom. The concept of a kingdom of God was not new to the Jews, although the exact phrase that we translate as kingdom wasn't found before Jesus.

In ancient days, the importance of kings in people's lives had molded their religious attitudes toward the idea of kingship. They formed their ideas about God around the human kings who ruled them. Moreover, because they had been known as *the chosen people,* the Israelites had long dreamed that they were destined for dominion in this world. To them the reign of God had grown to mean an earthly empire under God, ushered in by a Jewish warrior king type or messiah. This new world domain would be one in which the Jews ruled. They eventually looked back to the times of King David as the "golden age" and the pattern for the future kingdom.

In the meantime, there were some very serious national disasters that considerably influenced their beliefs. In a civil war, their nation was split in two, never to be united again; and then, after the Assyrian capture, ten of the twelve tribes of Israel were lost forever. Several hundred years later, the remaining two tribes were also captured by the Babylonians and were eventually subjected to the rule of the Persians, the Greeks, and then the Romans.

In spite of all this, they never lost their dream of the future kingdom they had come to believe in. But, because of the troubles they were having, they gradually developed a new concept of the *age to come* and of how the kingdom would finally come. They regarded whatever present age they were in as lost and bad. They came to believe that everything would have to get worse and worse until it couldn't get any worse, producing a period of woe. Then God would intervene and usher in the kingdom with vindication and glory for the Jews, establishing Israel as the world center and Jerusalem as the capital.

This was the background into which Jesus came, announcing that: " . . . *the kingdom of God is at hand.*" (Mark 1:5) We read in Luke 8:1 that: . . . *he went on through cities and villages, preaching and bringing the good news of the kingdom of God.*

Jesus developed His teaching out of the Old Testament heritage, but He saw how misguided the expectations of His fellow Jews had become and He arrived at a very different conclusion and brought forth an entirely new concept. He was not at all well understood by His contemporaries. Most of them listened to Him because they hoped and thought He was talking about the old kingdom they understood and expected. Therefore, He spent much time correcting the old beliefs prefaced by a statement like: *"You have heard that it was said . . . but I say to you."* (Matt. 5:21, 22) Apparently He was often asked (even by His own disciples) to be more literal and to pinpoint the kingdom. Usually He would reply to direct questions with an oblique answer saying: *"The kingdom of heaven is like . . . "* (Matt. 13:31) and then He would only allude to or poetically illustrate some hint of truth about it.

Later, the mention of both concepts concerning God's rule was translated into our English Bible according to our understanding of the word *kingdom,* connotating the rigid domain of a king and his subjects, which is unfortunate when associated with Jesus' idea of the kingdom of God and heaven; for this is only part of what He meant. The notion that the kingdom of heaven is a place up in the sky where you go if you're good, and that hell is the alternate destination down below, came to the fore during the Middle Ages as a means to frighten people into religion.

Jesus spoke of the kingdom 113 times, yet He

never specifically located it. Perhaps the closest Jesus ever came to making specific statements about the kingdom made clear that heaven is neither a place nor something in the future. His announcement: *"The kingdom of God is at hand,"* is recorded in three gospels. In Luke 17:20 He made it very clear: *"The kingdom of God is not coming with signs to be observed; nor will they say, 'Lo, here it is!' or, 'There!' for behold, the kingdom of God is in the midst of you."*

To the Jews and Christians the kingdom was always "to come" or something in the future. But to Jesus, the kingdom is at hand, an ever-present dimension of Spirit, and literally within all people at all times. It was His recurring theme that the kingdom of God is within you here and now!

This is the most revolutionary teaching ever presented—the secret of the ages—a fundamental truth of existence that can stir and completely change every human heart and every human life. However, few people through the ages have even grasped its full significance. We have long sought the secret of the ages—the key to the power that controls the universe and our lives and destinies along with it.

A famous legend puts it very well. It tells how the gods were discussing where to hide the top secret to life so that man wouldn't discover it until he was mature enough not to misuse it. They thought of placing it on the highest mountain; then they thought of the bottom of the ocean or the furthermost parts. Finally they thought of the perfect place: they would hide it within man himself, because that would be the last place he would look.

It is amazing how true this legend has been. We have searched the Earth high and low. We have even reached out to the stars and outer space to unlock secrets. But it is time that our scientists begin a concerted search of inner space. The scientific process, which has unveiled to us many of the secrets of the world we are in, now needs to be directed to the much bigger world within us. Perhaps we have avoided or postponed this search because we are afraid to look deep within ourselves, afraid of what we will find because of the dim view we have been taught about ourselves.

It is our emotions that we seem to fear most. Our unmastered, uncontrolled feelings are what the bizarre imageries in books such as Revelation are really about. These feelings often play so much havoc in our lives, making our inner worlds seem more to us like *habitats of dragons* than a repository for the treasures of God's kingdom in us. Up to now, we would have preferred to blame it all on a devil rather than face ourselves. Many scientists now know that the new frontier is right within ourselves, dealing with the vast unexplored realms of human consciousness.

God has planted the seed of His own nature in each of us, the seed potential to express His very attributes, qualities, and powers. The mystery of the ages is simply that the Christ Spirit lives in each of us and is expressed through our minds, hearts, and lives—when we believe in Christ. Christ in you is your hope of glory. Heaven is simply living in the awareness of the God Spirit in us and letting this Christ Spirit rule. Heaven is really a state of consciousness. Most of us experience very little consciousness of heaven now because we believe in the wrong things. We are external-minded—we think small, we feel small, and we live small.

Jesus brought into the world a whole new idea, not only about God but about humanity. He revealed to us the light of spiritual Truth about our own divine potential.

As I said, very few people in Jesus' day had any idea what He was talking about when He said: " . . . the kingdom of God is in the midst of you." (Luke 17:21) (Or, within you as reported in the King James Version of the Bible.) Most religions emphasize just the opposite—the unworthiness, the insignificance, the fallibility, the flawed character of humanity, and that heaven and the creative power of God are outside us.

This was not Jesus' good news message. The real work of religion should be to support people in learning to develop their divine dimensions—to work, and let the Father within do His work. The kingdom of God is within you, and it is a wondrous world. It is the source of everything spiritual—divine intelligence, infinite power, all-supplying abundance, and universal love.

Heaven, which means "expansion," is the bringing forth of the kingdom. It is a state of mind that unfolds your potential. The kingdom is, therefore, a higher, expanding expression that comes about from a changing, growing, expanding consciousness. Remember when Jesus once said: *"Blessed are the poor in spirit, for theirs is the kingdom of heaven"*? (Matt. 5:3) He was telling us that an open, receptive, teachable mind is the channel through which our spiritual potential manifests.

If you can't believe or even grasp the glorious idea of the infinite potential available within you (perhaps because of the staggering implications), surely you can at least accept as true that there is a lot more in you and to you than anyone yet knows about or that you have ever used.

Heaven has always had some association with paradise or a state of bliss. To be in heaven can mean many things. But it will always involve experiencing and expressing some aspect or quality of the goodness of God that is already a part of your essential being. Heaven is realizing that you are a child of God with wonderful spirit potential indwelling you; indeed you are a unique being with your own infinite talent. In fact, knowing as the Scripture says: *Beloved, we are God's children now; it does not yet appear what we shall be. . . .* (I John 3:2)

Heaven is a learning experience, an expanding consciousness of God's good. It is the increasing awareness of God's heavenly qualities of peace, truth, beauty, friendship, and love. Learning can be one of the greatest joys in life; and the kingdom of heaven comes through study, observation, and prayer.

Heaven is a feeling of joy or conscious bliss that comes from experiencing these wonderful qualities of the good life within ourselves. Heaven is freedom, the true freedom to rise above where you now are—your present fears, confusion, and feelings of inadequacy. It is the freedom to plan for a better life, to dream of better things, to think higher, more Christlike thoughts, to love with the love of God so that God's infinite intelligence, love, goodness, and spiritual power reign in the kingdom of your consciousness.

Like life itself, heaven is an unfolding process, ever-evolving upward and onward. Therefore, at our present level, none of us experiences all these qualities at any one time. But each of us can experience some of heaven every day and keep it growing.

Literally, the kingdom of God is within you, a kingdom of spiritual possibilities that can and will fulfill the highest and best in your eternal life. The kingdom comes by the process of growth and unfoldment, which we accelerate as we establish the reign of God's Truth in our minds and hearts, and let it rule. When we let God's indwelling Spirit reign over all the purposes and concerns of our lives, we abide in heaven.

We will continue, in the following chapter, to interpret Jesus' teachings about God's indwelling kingdom for our personal level of understanding at our present time and place in life. This is what Jesus meant us to do. This is why He presented His message in the form of timeless parables, miracles, and the everyday activities of His own life, so that His message could convey to all of us the Truth we need at any time.

So remember, as we continue to explore what Jesus really taught, that He was introducing you to that wonder world within you—the realm of your spiritual potential. And remember that as a child of God it is your privilege, your birthright, and your duty to more and more bring forth and live in a quality of life called heaven.

Stop! Look! Listen!

Continuing to explore what Jesus really taught, let us begin to alert ourselves to the hidden Truth of His message. We have established that the central theme of all He taught is what the Bible calls the kingdom of God or heaven. We have seen what the concept of the kingdom meant to the Jews before the time of Jesus—how it started with the kind of relationship the ancient Hebrews had come to know under the old-time earthly kings and rulers, gradually being translated into their religious concepts.

Largely because of the succession of national disasters and conquests they had suffered under other people, the Jewish idea of the kingdom of God had grown into a dream in which, after things got so bad they couldn't get any worse, God would intervene. They thought God would send a messiah or savior, whom they pictured as a warrior king. They felt this king would usher in a kingdom on Earth under God—a world empire in which the Jewish people from then on would have world dominion, with Israel as the world center and Jerusalem as its capital.

Jesus had seen how misguided this concept had become, and, using the framework of the Old Testament notion, He introduced a totally new idea of the reign of God—a spiritual concept in which a completely new understanding was and is necessary. He knew people needed a spiritual understanding so they could comprehend the nature of God in spirit and Truth and could perceive that behind the visible, manifest world there is an invisible realm of Spirit—a kingdom of God's infinite spiritual being that is the essence of all existence.

Most revolutionary of all, He introduced a new understanding of humanity in the light of spirit and Truth that included a recognition of our essential spiritual nature and our spiritual relationship to all creation as children of God, created in the image and likeness of God.

His message was that the kingdom is here, it always has been and always will be. The kingdom is also within us. In each of us dwells God's Spirit—the indwelling Christ or our latent higher Self, which most of us know so little about but which contains the nucleated whole or infinite Spirit as each ocean drop contains the relative whole of the ocean.

The great Truth Jesus revealed to us is that each of us is an infinitude—divine in origin, spiritually whole and complete in ourselves, lacking only the individual consciousness of our oneness with God, the source of all intelligence, power, and Spirit. In other words, as He said, those who

116

have eyes see, and those who have ears hear—inspirationally and intuitively. Jesus was revealing an entirely new concept of life, a spiritual perspective of God, the world, and especially of ourselves and our unique role in God's great plans and purposes for the universe.

He was giving us the *keys to the kingdom* and the spiritual insight into the spiritual working behind the universe. But spiritual things must be spiritually discerned. Jesus knew His kingdom message would only be grasped by a few, so He planted His teachings like seeds in parables. He knew that these simple, little, earthly stories could keep their heavenly truths safe and intact until individuals from then on achieved the illumined consciousness that would reveal the hidden spiritual lessons.

We read in Matthew 13:34: *All this Jesus said to the crowd in parables; indeed he said nothing to them without a parable. This was to fulfill what was spoken by the prophet: "I will open my mouth in parables, I will utter what has been hidden since the foundation of the world."* But even His own disciples came to Him after He had told the parable of the sower to a great multitude and asked Him: *"Why do you speak to them in parables?"* And His answer was, *"This is why I speak to them in parables, because seeing they do not see, and hearing they do not hear, nor do they*

117

understand." (Matt.13:13)

The religions that grew out of Jesus' teachings have not completely understood Jesus' spiritual concepts of the kingdom either, even though He placed such emphasis on the idea that the kingdom of heaven is at hand (not " *'Lo here, or lo there,'* " but within), that it comes by growth and expansion from within like a seed or like leaven. Indeed, the word *heaven* means expansion. In spite of this, the churches have taught that heaven is a place up in the sky where we go after we die, if we have been "good" and belong to the right church.

This does bring up a point for those of us (and this includes most of us) who have been taught the traditional religious concept of a heaven in the sky complete with pearly gates and streets of gold. If that isn't true, and the kingdom of heaven is within, in fact is not a place at all but a level of consciousness, what happens to us after we die? Jesus gave us ample encouragement about life beyond this one, but we must not confuse it with His total teachings about the kingdom. He said: *"In my Father's house are many rooms. . . ."* (John 14:2) The meaning here is that life is growth toward spiritual perfection, and that in God's vast eternal universe there are abundant opportunities and provisions for us to continue our spiritual evolution, with chance after chance to learn, to grow—to unfold our spiritual potential.

This is a far higher promise than the rather childish and primitive notion that we only get one chance with very unequal opportunities. What a dim view of a God of love. And, if we do make it, we reside in a static situation, sitting on a cloud, playing a harp. As Mark Twain said: *With so few people knowing how to play harps—it sounds like sheer hell.*

The Greek word meaning heaven is translated as "expansion" or "expanding potential." And quite seriously, if our so-called afterlife were devoid of the heavenly qualities of continuing growth and expansion, it would certainly be boring. *"In my Father's house are many rooms. . . ."* Where do we go? Through Einstein we have learned that there are more than three dimensions. Many rooms implies many dimensions. It is quite possible that some of them exist right here simultaneously with the three dimensions we observe; and undoubtedly, there are many, many more.

The thing to remember about what happens after you slip into the invisible is that you are a spiritual being—that is your identity forever, and you will dwell in the house of the Father forever. Life is a continuum, and we can safely trust God to supply our every need for everlasting life. The reason is simple: the kingdom of heaven is within you—and *wherever you are, God is.*

Now back to the kingdom of Spirit and expanding potential that Jesus taught. The key parable about the kingdom is about the seed and the sower. This parable establishes the basic truth that the kingdom comes from what is sown—established—within our hearts by the law of growth and unfoldment.

Preliminary to that, in all of Jesus' parables is the caveat: *"He who has ears, let him hear."* Also, as Jesus said to His disciples in regard to the spiritual relationship of the Father and the Son: *"Blessed are the eyes which see what you see! For I tell you that many prophets and kings desired to see what you see, and did not see it, and to hear what you hear, and did not hear it."* (Luke 10:23, 24)

Certainly, the disciples at that time didn't really understand Jesus' kingdom message. What did they hear and see that had never truly been revealed before? The answer is Jesus Himself, or the Word made flesh. They heard what He taught with their physical ears, and they saw what He demonstrated with their physical eyes. At first their perception was all on this level. Once, He was asked, after He had talked so much about the subject of the Father: *"Lord, show us the Father, and we shall be satisfied."* (John 14:8) We have heard you talk about Him, but show Him to us and that will be enough. And Jesus said: *"Have I been with you so long, and yet you do not know me, Philip? He who has seen me has seen the Father . . . ."*

He might have added: "Haven't you seen how I have affirmed life, peace, health, prosperity, and all the blessings of life more abundant that come from the Father within? Haven't you seen how I overcame all manner of evil with good through the way of spiritual growth and mastery and how I have loved you? This is the Father—the indwelling spirit of God in action—manifest and made visible. This is the Word made flesh."

For ages, people have asked questions about God: Who is He? What is He like? Where do we look for Him? God can be known! We are designed with the ability to increasingly learn to know and to understand Him. Our spiritual evolution is linked to our evolution of understanding God. For what we believe He is at any particular time is what we tend to be like at that time.

We have long looked to the visible world to understand God. In the wonders of nature there is much visible evidence of the spiritual operation of God in action—the outworkings of the forces, the principles, the eternal order, and the supreme intelligence that govern the universe.

But the stars, for example, as well as many other of the scenes of nature, can tend to make

God seem remote, outside and beyond us—even inaccessible. Then, too, we are looking to discover God through human eyes that are limited to third dimension perspective and reflect our present level of awareness, which has often been distorted by human experience. The nature of anything—for us—is determined by our thought about it. The notion of an avenging God of wrath and eternal punishment that persists in some religions came from the ancient, primitive concepts our early ancestors formed by being subjected to that type of rulership under human kings.

To discover God through what we now see in the world and what we have humanly experienced in life is inadequate. It doesn't present a true picture. But since Jesus Christ came into the world, no one ever needs to be confused about the nature and character of God. Jesus revealed the whole Truth. In Him we witness God's spiritual nature unified with the human, for He is the image of the invisible God.

But Jesus told us that new wine cannot be put into old skins. For example, one time an Italian photographer was commissioned to travel all over the United States and take pictures so that people in Italy could know what America was like. Do you know what his pictures were? Everywhere in the portraits of people, the countryside, and the American city life, his eye had unconsciously looked for what was familiar to him. He didn't see America at all. His pictures were of Italy!

Jesus made great provisions in His teachings for our overcoming of this primary obstacle of locked-in vision and closed minds. He said: " . . . *unless one is born anew, he cannot see the kingdom of God.*" (John 3:3) God reveals Himself according to our receptivity. Spiritual things must be spiritually discerned. Spiritual rebirth essentially is the experience associated with our innate capacity to depart from the old, strictly human, third dimensional, mundane perception and open our awareness to the things of Spirit. It is an awakening—an inner change—a conversion to a higher understanding so that we catch the vision—see and hear from the point of view of Jesus Christ. Then we are blessed with ears that hear and eyes that see.

The most important thing for us to change is our picture of God, which then changes everything else. The right knowledge of God is emphasized by Jesus. First, He showed us the Father (in His own life), and then He told us that we must come to understand God " . . . *in spirit and truth . . .* " (John 4:24) which opens our perception to the spiritual significance of all things. As a result, we gain new insights from the commonplace subjects of His parables, like grass, flowers, birds, seeds, harvests, money, clothing, home, and the *far country*. He was telling us that, if we start with a

123

true spiritual concept of God as a loving, benevolent, all-good heavenly Father, we will then discover the world, ourselves, and the true meaning of life in a wonderful new light.

His parables were designed to help in our rebirth, to awaken, change, and make us new from within with intuitive flashes and new insights of the eternal Truth. They were constructed to lift our vision of life and open our ears, eyes, and hearts to Jesus' spiritual concepts.

Always remember that to know something is not to be bound by it. Spiritual growth is an inner evolution into new levels of consciousness. The great secret in understanding Jesus is to learn to listen for the spiritual implications and the underlying truth in everything He taught and would have us observe. We must learn to see all things in terms of their spiritual unity and their oneness—to realize the connection between the invisible "within" and the visible "without," and to simultaneously see things whole. In His teachings, Jesus would have us Stop! Look! and Listen! All of life is waiting to reveal its Truth. The world is full of Truth, good, love, and beauty.

Several centuries ago Brother Lawrence, a monk, was doing K.P. in a monastery kitchen. He was inspired in the midst of all the pots and pans with the idea of *practicing the presence of God*. To me this means learning to stop right where you are at any time and look and listen for evidence of the presence, power, and activity of God right then and there.

A great help in learning to grow into spiritual awareness is to practice translating every important thing in your life into its spiritual equivalent. This can be done with anything you want in your life—health, peace, harmony, success, prosperity, friendship, love, and happiness. There is a spiritual cause and source right within you for everything you need in your life. It will respond to your recognition and your mental support of it, and it will quicken, under its own power, the activity that will begin to bring it forth in your life.

Every day, pause and go apart awhile in prayer and meditation, look from the vantage point of *the secret place of the most high,* and listen to the still small voice. And you will learn secrets hidden from the foundation of the world.

God's Assured Outcome

I would like to remind everyone that within each of us is a deep need to feel that our life has been worthwhile, that it has counted, and that somehow and in some way the world is a little better because we have lived in it. Perhaps the saddest lament possible is from someone who feels that his or her life has not been worth much.

The truth is that every day you have ever lived will someday fall into place—each moment will have counted for something. This is the "judgment day" concept; and, in reality, every day is judgment day because every day's moments, thoughts, words, and feelings do count.

This is all true because this universe exists for a purpose and with a plan. We are a part of that purpose, and that plan is constantly working out its deep design in us—and often, friends, in spite of us. But this too is the plan. With our God-given gift of free choice, we are free at any time to cooperate with the plan or to considerably thwart it. But we can never defeat it, because some part of that plan is always at work in us evolving that image God had in His mind when He created us in His likeness.

The good news is that every thought, word, and action we use in accord with that plan (or what we call Truth) will add its increase and contribute toward fulfilling the promise of that plan in us. In the *"way and the truth"* of the Christ life, there is no grand nor inferior; there is nothing insignificant. God's plan is built into every phase of His creation, and the outcome is assured. This is especially good to know right now, because we are going through a very special time of change— a world-changing quantum leap—from within.

Much is still on the invisible side, but new energies are now in action. On the inner plane, powerful forces are breaking up old patterns and inspiring accelerated revisions in human thinking that will elevate the consciousness of all and help bring forth a new age. Yet the effects of this momumental inner reformation are beginning to be felt everywhere—from the international scene with changes in China and the Mideast, right down the line to every individual. Changes in the nation, economy, weather, and church are increasing drastically, and they are affecting everyone.

In order to make room for the consciousness of the new age, old and often cherished concepts are being put away. Because we are in the midst of this dramatic transformation, this is a time of uncertainty. Almost everyone seems to be somewhat restless or even troubled. If you are having uneasy or disturbing feelings and/or experiences, remember that you are not alone. The whole world is going through this change, and it is just the dark before a great dawn with an assured outcome.

Before we talk about how to incorporate these powerful, benevolent energies into our lives and cooperate as fully as possible with the plan behind them, let me establish two things for background. First, I would like to convince all of us (at least intellectually) that great changes in human life not only can happen but already have. We are still in the dynamics of such a change brought about by what we call *science*. Science has come close to being our God in the sense that we have accepted it, believed in it, and come to depend on it for much of our health, wealth, happiness, and security. Science has come to rule our world, and for about three decades the balance of world power has hinged on our daily progress in science. Science, of course, is only a body of knowledge or a system of gathering knowledge. It disciplines itself (very rigidly) to observing only what is seen, felt, weighed, and measured, continually exploring and testing new things, no matter where they lead. Therefore, science has maintained a marvelous quality of progress that has never existed in religion.

In science, dogma and doctrine have been replaced (or transcended) by a self-correcting, everchanging quest for objective fact. We have been living in a dynamic scientific revolution. One-half

129

of all the discoveries and inventions from the beginning of human history have been made in the past fifty years—they have doubled every ten years.

In the first beatitude, *"Blessed are the poor in spirit,"* Jesus told us that in order to advance, we must be willing to "die" to old concepts so that we can be reborn to new ideas.

After some incredible religious persecution, the first major change in scientific thinking hinged around Copernicus' new idea that the Earth is a sphere that rotates around the sun. We finally died to the old concept that the Earth was flat and the fixed center of the universe. For example, the old theory, based on the flat-Earth concept, once stated that the Earth stood still, which is of course how it would have appeared. But we now know better than that.

The great breakthrough directly involved uncertainty. It was Heisenburg's "Principle of Uncertainty" by which we finally learned (just as Jesus had said) that we are not to judge by appearances, that we cannot really trust what we see and feel and measure with our five senses. We once believed that we lived in a fixed, rigid universe of solid objects existing in vast oceans of nothingness. Instead, we live in a dynamic, alive, moving, ever-changing universe that will not "stand still" to be measured—with the uncertainty being that, if we concentrate our attention on one thing, we lose our perspective about everything else. But, rather ironically, this apparent limitation to the understanding we used to have, which was probably confusing and disturbing at first, actually introduced us into the nuclear age. For this new concept made it possible for Einstein to formulate the Theory of Relativity and give us a new cosmic understanding of the universe.

Relativity means the relatedness of all things, the system of cooperation by which everything in the universe is related in an ultimate unity. This is a universe of many dimensions, expressed in infinite variations; as Jesus said: *"In my Father's house are many rooms. . . ."* (John 14:2) All things are from but one substance—radiant energy—containing one intelligence, one purpose, one plan, one creative, directing motive-force ever evolving toward a cosmic wholeness. In other words, we have discovered that this is a holistic or whole-producing universe in which two things always produce a third thing that is greater than the sum of the original parts. This is the scientific discovery of what Unity teaches: one Presence, one Power, one essential Nature—Good—bringing all things right and working all things together for good in the universal unity of love. This revolutionary scientific discovery also led us to discover more of the mysteries of the universe, not only in the vastness we can observe in outer space or the without, but within, to the tiniest of things, so small it can't be seen—the atom, and now the quark.

We who long associated greatness with bigness learned that God always works from the "small." Everything in His universe is as great in miniature as in magnitude—there is no *less*. From this we learned that there is a within as well as a without to life, and the within gives rise to the without according to strict, dependable rules. Emerson once said: *God's dice are loaded* (for Good). But Einstein said: *God doesn't play dice*. Nothing is left to chance. Everything works from center to circumference, from the within to the without, under a direct relationship between cause and effect, the high vision of an infallible creation.

The scientific knowledge of the last fifty years has collapsed the old "three-decker" concept of the universe (of Earth here, heaven up there, and hell down there) around which many people still base their religious beliefs. In ways that would defy the wonders and dreams of our ancestors, it has rolled back a lot of darkness and drastically changed the course of civilization by giving us an entirely new working understanding into the inner activities of our physical universe. Here is where science leaves off; and I suppose it should, for this is not an essentially physical universe—it is a spiritual universe.

We have had three chapters about Jesus' spiritual concepts of the universe—His explanation of the inner workings of creation that He called the kingdom of God, the infinite realm of God's spiritual essence, above and beyond our world of time and space yet ever-present, permeating everything—eternally at hand and within. Jesus plainly stated that: *"The kingdom of God is in the midst [within] you"* (Luke 17:20)—a kingdom of heaven, meaning an inner domain of expanding spiritual potential. He told us that the kingdom comes by letting God's spiritual influence increasingly come into our minds and hearts, and work in our lives.

The greatest discovery in the universe is that God is all there is and that we were created in God to express what God is. We are now incomplete, from an earthly point of view. Yet, everyone is a spiritual being, a child of God, created with the potential of expressing the nature of the Father.

The second part of helpful background information is to understand what Jesus meant when He said: *"The kingdom of God is like a grain of mustard seed."* (Matt. 13:31) What a beautifully simple yet profound way to introduce us to our own destiny and God's assured outcome of what He created us to be.

A seed is something small that can grow to incredible proportions because of the hidden potential wrapped up in it waiting to be awakened. Some of the most majestic forces in the universe are called in to make a tiny mustard seed grow. A seed, any seed, is a center of energy, a sleeping bundle of creativity. All we have to do is plant it and help make sure it has a chance to grow. And then, by natural sequence the seed unfolds and develops from its center by the law of life, which is growth. This great principle is the key to the mystery of all life.

Jesus was constantly telling and showing us that the truly important things in life start seed-small and unfold by orderly growth from the little seed to a bountiful harvest. God's assured outcomes, which are the real miracles of the universe, are locked and sealed into every tiny seed.

And this, perhaps, is the greatest wonder of all. Each seed not only contains the potential to grow from infinitesimal beginnings to a magnificent harvest, but each seed also contains a built-in pattern—perfection—that is the promise of its fulfillment of what God intended it to be. A mustard seed will always become a mustard plant, and never anything else! Acorn, rhubarb, watermelon—every kind of seed planted and cultivated always turns out as intended by God—the results are inevitable.

We, as any other seed, have a built-in pattern of

perfection—the Christ seed. The growth of this seed begins and proceeds in our minds and hearts. When we let God's influence into our consciousness, even as the smallest seed of Truth, the leavening power of His nature in us can expand, uplift, and transform our lives. The quickened spiritual influence is irrepressible. Emerson was right when he said: *God's dice are loaded,* in that that which is good grows—slowly perhaps, but everything counts!

Every day, by unfailing law, every good, positive, constructive thought, word, or deed of your life produces after its kind and has an influence and a destiny beyond itself. What a difference a little faith, gratitude, patience, tolerance, understanding, love, and prayer can make. What a difference one little breakthrough can make in evolving everyone to a new higher level. It only took one—Einstein. What a difference any little improvement can make in our own personal consciousness—one positive, loving thought can transmute thousands that have been negative.

A young boy won an art prize in an exhibit, and when someone congratulated him on having such a good picture, he said, "It isn't my best drawing." When he was asked why he hadn't exhibited his best drawing, he answered, "Oh, my best drawing isn't drawn yet."

The boy was on his way to becoming a real

artist. In you is the power to become what God intended you to be. The attainment will come by growth. It all comes back to the quality of the thoughts and feelings that you chose to entertain and maintain in your consciousness day by day and minute by minute. Charles Fillmore said: *All we have to do to change our life is to start thinking along the Jesus Christ lines.*

There is an all-powerful spiritual influence ready at all times to help you fulfill God's plan in you. And there is no *less*. Where you are right now is exactly the right place for you to begin the rest of eternal life. Get started. Begin with the very next thought to align your thinking to the Jesus Christ standard; the results are assured—inevitable.

Pierre Teilhard de Chardin, former priest and scientist, believed as we do in universal unity and in God's assured outcomes. From his "The Phenomenon of Man," we get an answer to the old gloom-and-doom concept of a flawed humanity: *Man is irreplaceable. Therefore, however improbable it might seem, he must reach the goal, not necessarily, doubtless, but infallibly.*

It's a Miracle!

I'm sure that all of us at times wish that a miracle could take place in our lives. There are times when we may feel that a miracle is the only thing that can help us. Miracles do happen! The life of Jesus is often most dramatically associated with miracles. The Bible says that this is the way He originally displayed His divine power and awakened His disciples' faith in Him.

The miracles of Jesus began at a wedding in which He transformed water into wine. This event is a significant story and covers an important lesson. It was the first activity of Jesus' ministry. After His baptism and the temptations, He went to Galilee with His disciples, apparently for a short visit with His mother, Mary. She greeted them with good news: they had all been invited to a wedding at Cana.

In those days a wedding feast was the most important social event in the lives of the people. It was the one event that could bring laughter and gaiety into lives that were most often hard, bleak, and austere. Large weddings, therefore, often lasted as long as a week, and a great deal of food and drink had to be provided. This was furnished by the guests with a definite order of protocol in which the older guests presented their food and wine first and the young followed in descending sequence.

Apparently, Jesus and His party arrived late in the week, and the provisions were running low. Mary pointed this out to Jesus. He, at first, seemed reluctant; but Mary persisted by telling the servants to do whatever Jesus told them to do. Then Jesus transformed water into wine so that the wedding could continue.

First of all, this was an act of lovingkindness. To run out of wine at the wedding would have been a lifelong humiliation to the bride and groom. They would have lost face—the worst social tragedy in the East.

Christians have sometimes had trouble with the idea of the wine. There is a story about a fundamental Christian who was lecturing someone about drinking. The man said: "Jesus drank wine." And the religionist said, "Yes, and I would have thought a lot more of Him if He hadn't."

There is also a story about someone who used this event to his own advantage. His name was Pat and he had a problem with drinking. He took the pledge, but he "slipped." With a bottle in his hand, he ran right into the priest. The good father said, "Pat, what's in that bottle?" And Pat answered, "Just water, Father." The priest asked to smell it, and then said: "Pat, that's wine." And Pat said, "Faith and begorra, Jesus Christ has pulled off another fantastic miracle!"

The lesson of the Bible story has nothing to do with drinking wine. We need to get past the literal interpretation of the story or we will never grasp its true meaning. Within the story itself are symbols. Symbols are the universal language of Spirit, and the true value of this story is found in its spiritual significance.

In the Bible, a wedding represents an inner union—a marriage between two complementary internal processes in us that produces a positive, constructive attitude. On the psychological level, it is the right combination of thoughts and feelings. Glenn Clark once illustrated this in a story about "hind's feet."

A young man who was struggling in life met a very wealthy and successful man on a train. When the young man asked about the secret of his success, the older man replied, "Hind's feet." The young man searched for several years for the secret of the symbology and eventually found the older man again. This time he explained it: "There is a type of mountain goat that has the ability, when walking on narrow, dangerous mountain passages, to place his hind foot exactly in the same footing where his front foot had been. Other animals cannot do that, so they often tumble down the mountain." The old man's secret of success was that he was able to place his feelings and

141

emotions exactly behind the intellectual and mental images; and that brought his success.

This is an important thing to know about your formative power of thought. It is the idea behind what we now call "success motivation."—establishing positive thoughts behind our own goals. It is important to have goals, for they mobilize and give direction to our consciousness. But there is an even higher way that our minds can function. Through intuition and inspiration, the truly creative mind action draws directly on the fount of infinite intelligence and transforms our ordinary consciousness. We are lifted into inspired new levels of expanded awareness that exceed the limits of anything we can plan or accomplish with our normal rational-deductive-intellectual thinking. Paul stated the true goal we should all aspire to: . . . *the goal for the prize of the upward call of God in Christ Jesus.* (Phil. 3:14) Anything less than this is diluted "wine" and eventually runs out.

Let's look at the story in this light. The wedding symbolizes a spiritual union within us—a marriage between the natural human side and the spiritual side, which is our true nature. Certainly, this idea's time has come, for we are now entering the new age in which we will really begin to live from our spiritual potential. *Water,* in the Bible, can have several meanings—one is external cleansing. Another meaning is the concept of unlimited possibilities. It can also mean unsteady, *as unstable as water,* which in this story symbolizes the state of the natural human life. *Wine* means spiritual life. When the wine runs low, it is lacking the vitalizing power of Spirit—it is flat and tasteless or run down.

The ruler of the feast is that part of us that is in charge of our natural, human level of life—the goals, motivations, and concepts of our strictly human consciousness. Mary, the mother of Jesus, represents the purest, highest emotion that we can experience—intuition—which prepares the way for the Christ power to follow. Jesus, as He always does in the Bible, represents the Christ—the I AM Spirit of God in man—the miracle-working power of the universe in each of us. The disciples represent the twelve powers or faculties of man—the potential to become spiritualized in us. The servants at the wedding represent the part of our human personality and intelligence that can respond to intuition. This represents a change in our level of dependence from things of the world to the source or the kingdom of Spirit. We can then obey and serve the indwelling Christ Spirit.

Jesus, at first, was a guest at the wedding. His mother, Mary, who had wholehearted confidence in Him, began to instruct the servants to do whatever Jesus told them to do. The conversation between Jesus and His mother seems a little harsh:

143

"O woman, what have you to do with me? My hour has not yet come." (John 2:4) Jesus had utmost tenderness and regard for His mother. *"My hour has not yet come"* refers to the order of protocol in which the older guests were first. But Mary knew that the wedding was breaking down, life's wine was running out. She knew it was time for Jesus, the guest, to become the Master of the feast.

Jesus then instructed the servants to pour water into six stone jars; and then it became wine. Not only wine, but good wine—the best!—as the old ruler of the feast very quickly recognized and appreciated. The three symbols—water, stone jars, and good wine—give us the levels of mind action involved in the miraculous transformation. Water is the natural intellectual level, a level by which most of us live almost all the time—a level that, by itself, is unstable and inadequate for the truly full life. The jars of stone represent filling our thoughts and feelings with literal truth. That is, the intellectual discipline of a program of study of spiritual Truth and higher knowledge—what we call being a Truth student.

There were six stone jars—a numerical symbol of the Jewish Rite of Purification—which can mean prayer and meditation. The number six corresponds to the first six days of the week of creation in which we work, the seventh being that segment of the creative process in which the Father does His miracle-producing work.

A miracle is an experience of Truth or the transformation that occurs in our nature when Truth comes alive in us. Miracles do not suspend the laws of the universe, they elevate them. The miracle of miracles is the new person we can become and the new life we can live when the Christ Spirit becomes a living part of us and lifts us upward into our divine potential. A miracle of self-change occurs.

I again would like to mention study, prayer, and meditation—they are vital avenues for this life-changing process. We usually associate miracles with instantaneous events, such as Paul's blinding encounter with the living Christ on the road to Damascus. But these in themselves don't last—they run out. Spiritual transformation is a growing and cumulative process. It needs constant study, prayer, and meditative support. So long as Christ is but a guest in our consciousness, our lives deplete and go flat again. When Christ truly becomes Master, and when we live in a growing awareness of the radiant presence of the living Christ in us, then we increasingly experience the results of the growing union or marriage between the two sides of our nature. That union is the blending of the human with the divine in the right relationship in which Spirit governs the human.

The miracles never cease! As we study, pray, and meditate, higher levels in ourselves progressively open and become active, and new qualities come forth. Strange and wonderful things keep happening. We receive new inspiration, new enlightenment, new awareness that bring into our lives new experiences of exciting, adventurous living. Good wine is equal to creative living and is superior to anything we have known. It is always available to everyone but still hidden from most.

Religion has often been grim and gloomy. The imagery of wine tells us that life is meant to be enjoyed. In this story, the old, harsh John the Baptist religion of external water cleansing (repent, or else) is replaced by a new religion of Spirit that says: " . . . *be of good cheer, I have overcome the world.*" (John 16:33) As Paul said: . . . *rejoice in our hope of sharing the glory of God.* (Rom. 5:2) Miracles happen! They can happen in your life! When you open your mind to His spiritual influence, God can display His divine power, His glory in your life. Again, the great Truth, the . . . *mystery, which is Christ in you, the hope of glory.* (Col. 1:27)

Here is what Charles Fillmore said about the wedding at Cana: *Spiritually, marriage represents the union of two dominant states of consciousness. When we open the door of the mind by consciously affirming the presence and power of the divine I AM in our midst, there is a marriage or union of the higher forces in being with the lower and we find that we are quickened in every part; the life of the I AM has been poured out for us.*

Jesus promises in this story that there is no situation in your life that cannot be transformed by the I AM power of the Christ in you. And an even better promise is that the best years of your life can be now and in all the nows to come. Charles Fillmore was 93 years old when he wrote: *I fairly sizzle with zeal and enthusiasm as I spring forth to do the things that ought to be done by me.* Why? How? Because he discovered and began to live out the Christ in himself by making the study of Truth and prayer, and above all, meditation, the highest priorities in his life!

Every day he filled his consciousness with Truth. He prayed often. The most important event of his entire day was the time he spent in the holy of holies, the secret place—the silence of his mind.

Do you want a miracle in your life? You can have an abundance of them if you will follow the instructions Jesus gave for miracles at the wedding at Cana, and if you will do what Charles Fillmore did by making the study of Truth, prayer, and meditation the highest priorities in your life!

The Secret of Your Personal Power

Life, to many people, is what happens to them while they are making other plans. Think of that. To these people, life is a backwater experience in which they are capriciously buffeted around by whatever comes into their lives. But it doesn't have to be that way!

Jesus came to reveal " . . . *the way, and the truth, and the life*" (John 14:6)—a way in which we can live directly from the Source; a way in which we can be drawn right into the mainstream of life and placed on the crest of the wave of the infinite creative process that is continually unfolding itself in all the universe.

Now, think again about yourself. Is life something happening to you while you make other plans? Typically, most of our plans, dreams, and expectations are of *this* world. But Jesus' message was about another domain, a transcendent realm which He said is *not* of this world. Jesus came to show us how to live from all our resources, the way God created us to live.

The central theme of His message to us was based on a concept we have translated into English as the *kingdom*—the kingdom of God or the kingdom of heaven. There is little doubt about the importance of this kingdom to Jesus. He mentioned it 113 times in the short record we have about Him in the Gospels. Yet never once did Jesus define the kingdom literally. Instead, He presented His message in the poetry of parables or precepts, comparing the qualities and activities of the kingdom with seeds, leaven, fishnets, pearls, talents, and weddings. This was because His message is about a spiritual kingdom—the infinite realm of God's Spirit that is everlastingly within and readily at hand. Jesus knew and often predicated what He taught with the qualification that spiritual things must be spiritually discerned. Spiritual insight provides the breakthrough to understanding the truth of Jesus Christ.

His fellow Jews, including His own disciples, thought Jesus was talking about the long-awaited religious-political kingdom (like that of David) that Judaism had grown to expect. This kingdom was to be ushered in by a warrior king who would overthrow the Romans, establishing Israel in its place of sovereign world leadership under God. Later, the Christian theologians formulated the idea (around the term *eschatology*) that heaven was an after-life reward—a place in the sky that we go to if we belong to the right religion. This was a misconception that Jesus had already corrected when He had been asked by the Pharisee, "When is the kingdom coming?" And He had said: *"The kingdom of God is not coming with signs to be ob-*

served; nor will they say 'Lo, here it is!' or 'There!' for behold, the kingdom of God is in the midst of you." [within you] (A.V.) (Luke 17:20) And what ingenious ways we have used in our theology to miss the point about that!

The spiritual understanding necessary to discern a spiritual message takes us out of the third dimensional world in which most of us live. It lifts us right out of the realm of time and space into another domain. The kingdom of God is not a physical location; it is the omnipresent, ever-pervading spiritual dimension of life. And for each of us the kingdom of heaven is the indwelling possibility of God's spiritual nature planted in us when He created us. It is this spark of divinity, the Christ potential in each of us that Paul said is our . . . hope of glory. (Col. 1:27)

Jesus used a variety of terms to reveal this inner spiritual dimension to us. His most endearing name for God's infinite, abiding presence was Father. There were also poetic allusions to different aspects of the kingdom, such as truth, source, cause, and sonship. He illustrated its attributes in terms of its growing possibilities, transforming power, ruling influence, absolute goodness, and unfailing love. He always presented it as the ultimate value and meaning, the priceless divine element in all life. And everything He presented referred to a spiritual influence that can be brought into our own lives at any time, because God's nature is the essence of our very own being.

Another helpful way to consider the kingdom of heaven is as a state of consciousness—a domain of spiritual consciousness and a higher level of attainment that can be reached within ourselves. Jesus often emphasized the importance of our inner lives—the condition and quality of our minds and hearts. He reiterated the law of mind action (as within, so without) by which our spiritual unfoldment proceeds and grows from our hearts. Therefore, He admonished that our most important job is to establish and maintain high Christlike qualities within ourselves—in our own private, often hidden thoughts and feelings. To be in the kingdom means to be awakened to our spiritual possibilities and reborn into new levels of spiritual consciousness.

We see then that the key to the kingdom is in recognizing the as yet undiscovered spiritual potential that is locked in the very core of our own being and is drawing on and living from those divine possibilities that are always at hand and within.

In this chapter, we are going to explore the kingdom message around the frequently asked question, "When shall the kingdom come?"

If you remember, Jesus started the drama of His ministry by appearing on the scene at the age of about thirty, announcing that " . . . *the king-dom of God is at hand. . . .* " (Mark 1:15) Accompanying this were vivid examples of spiritual preparation through the events of His baptism, the temptations, and choosing His disciples. He then performed His first miracle at the wedding of Cana. Next, He talked to a man named Nicodemus. And then He had a conversation with the woman at the well. In this fallen woman, who seemed to be a barren field, He had seen the glory of a spiritual potential that could bloom into a beautiful life. To her, an audience of one person, He revealed one of the greatest Truths in life—the poetic living water of spiritual influence that can bring us truly alive from within ourselves. To this he added the immensely important exhortation that we must learn to worship in *spirit* and *truth*.

This story is a spiritual high point in Jesus' ministry and one of the truly great dramas of the Bible. As a result of her brief encounter with Jesus, the woman who had made a complete mess of her life was miraculously transformed and became a living, joyous, effervescent example of the awesome influence of the well of water springing up into eternal life. At this point in the story, His disciples, who had gone to get something to eat and had given Him the chance to talk to the woman, returned with food. When they found Jesus talking to a Samaritan woman they were chagrined, because such a thing was a definite social taboo in those days. Jesus used this point to teach them a very valuable lesson. As they approached Him they said: *"Rabbi, eat."* But He said to them, *"I have food to eat of which you do not know."* (John 4:31, 32) The disciples questioned each other: *"Has anyone brought him food?"* Jesus said to them, *"My food is to do the will of him who sent me, and to accomplish his work. Do you not say, 'There are yet four months, then comes the harvest'? I tell you, lift up your eyes and see how the fields are already white for harvest."* (John 4:34, 35) He then reiterated His teaching about sowing and reaping.

This story is found in the Gospel of John, which is a deeply metaphysical (spiritual-oriented) book. And it can only be understood spiritually; it makes no sense otherwise. Jesus' teachings, His consciousness, His mind, and His life were all on a completely different level from the average human being and the average religion. He had an entirely new interpretation and viewpoint of life—He beheld totally different values, different meanings, and different goals. He knew about a different process by which life is successfully lived; and it was His mission to reveal and exemplify this higher Truth.

When He said: . . . *"I have food . . . of which you do not know,"* Jesus was revealing how we

154

can enter into and draw upon the infinite, omni-present spiritual resource and begin to live as He did. It was one more way of saying: " . . . *the kingdom of God is in the midst of you."* *[within you.] (A.V.)* (Luke 17:21) Jesus was stating that the great nourishment in life, the thing that distin-guished Him so much and set Him apart, was from drawing on the kingdom within and doing the will of the One who sent Him. In other words, Jesus knew absolutely the great spiritual mission in His life and He allowed it to become His whole life. The only thing He cared about and thought about was to live out this great divine plan—to carry out God's will, God's great plan of good in His life.

And in doing this, the Christ nature (the Father in Him) was given full expression and, as Charles Fillmore once said, you couldn't tell in the life of Jesus where the human left off and the God began. Jesus protracted His personal example of the Christ life with the statement: " . . . *he who believes in me will also do the works that I do; and greater works than these will he do, because I go to the Father."* (John 14:12)

The tragedy in Christianity so far is that we have not yet understood that Jesus came to reveal the truth about us. He didn't come as a great excep-tion but as the great exemplification of the spiritual Truth about what is possible for *us* as the image and likeness of God. He told us about the great divine potential in each of us—the fields that are white for harvest waiting to express themselves.

God works through seeds—by the universal law of growth. Evolution is the great law of life. Everywhere you look, creation is evolving. Nothing stands still, nothing stays the same. Everything comes from an invisible essence within, growing from something small into something larger, unfolding an inherent potential that was designed and placed there by God. This was why Jesus illustrated the kingdom with stories about seeds. For example, all that a rose can ever be is initially in its seed. An acorn is a perfect oak in potential, yet unfulfilled in expression. To be fulfilled, it must grow according to the patterns of the seed. The most wonderful thing about a seed—any seed—is that it always fulfills its own unique role in creation; a rose seed always produces a rose, an acorn always becomes an oak.

The same is true of us. The seed of God is in us—the Christ pattern—and as God's image and likeness, we are predestined as junior partners in His creation. As with Jesus, there is a plan—a spiritual destiny—and a unique contribution to God's universal plan of good implanted in us (as latent talents and abilities) which unfolds the potential and grows from our essential nature—Christ in us.

156

Jesus told each of us that to begin to live the way He did, allowing the Father within to do His works, we need to discover God's plan for life (His will) and begin to live our entire lives for that plan. And when we do, we will draw, directly from the Source, upon that spiritual nourishment, the food He mentioned to His disciples.

Quite simply, Jesus told us that the way to live—the one way we were designed to live and the only way we can really live—is from center to circumference, by awakening to and unfolding the spiritual seed of our own divinity.

Jesus of course knew the human problems involved in initiating a life of spiritual unfoldment. He knew all the things that hold us back and keep us from entering into life as it was meant to be. To help us, He spoke of the insignificance of worldly rewards, our concern with harvesting what we plant, and He lifted our vision instead toward the prize of the high calling of Jesus Christ—the Christ life. The only concern is in doing what is ours to do today and trusting God to supply our daily bread in everything necessary for today's growth and spiritual welfare. Everything we need physically, mentally, emotionally, or spiritually, is prepared and waiting in God's infinite reservoir for the time we need it.

Another thing Jesus spoke about that holds us back is our impatience about getting what we want when we want it. The kingdom comes in an orderly sequence of spiritual growth: "... *first the blade, then the ear, then the full grain in the ear.*" (Mark 4:28)

As we move toward the secret of personal power, here is something to remember: anytime we attempt to achieve anything by personal force, we must maintain it by the same force. When we let up, so does it. But conversely, anything that we establish within God's plan is maintained by the infinite power of the universe. "When is the kingdom coming?" is not a matter so much of time, but of timing.

So, the first part of the secret of your personal power is to understand the importance of timing—not yours but God's.

From the book "Zorba the Greek" let's share an insight into what not to do—especially with our goals and values and concepts of rewards:

"I remember one morning when I discovered a cocoon in the bark of a tree, just as a butterfly was making a hole in its case and preparing to come out. I watched and waited awhile, but it was too long appearing and I was impatient. I bent over it and breathed on it to warm it. I warmed it as quickly as I could and the miracle began to happen before my eyes, faster than life. The case opened, the butterfly started slowly crawling out—and I shall never forget my horror when I saw how its wings were folded back and crumpled; the wretched butterfly tried with its whole trembling body to unfold them. Bending over it, I tried to help it with my breath, in vain. It needed to be hatched out patiently and the unfolding of the wings should be a gradual process in the sun. Now it was too late. My breath had forced the butterfly to appear, all crumpled, before its time. It struggled desperately and, a few seconds later, died in the palm of my hand. That little body is, I believe, the greatest weight I have on my conscience. For I realize that it is a mortal sin to violate the great laws of nature. We should not hurry, we should not be impatient, but we should confidently obey the eternal rhythm."

When it is time in God's plan for anything to happen, it will be brought forth the right way under its own power—and nothing can hold it back. It will be maintained by the self-renewing power of the infinite Spirit of God. If you feel you have done things in your life, maybe at least subtly for rewards, if you've worked and you think it should come, especially if an answer to prayer seems delayed, then it is probably God's way of telling you: "Wait! Things aren't ready yet. Be patient. Have I ever got a plan for you!"

This then is the second thing to understand about the secret of your personal success—God *has* a plan for you, and it is built right into your essential being. Know that everything you will ever need to meet, to overcome, and to grow into your next level of creative possibilities is already waiting to serve you at the right time and in the right way. You came into this life with everything you will ever need to live a full and spiritually successful life.

The secret of your personal success is in learning to bring the spiritual dimension of the kingdom of heaven into your everyday life—drawing each day, from the source in you, the spiritual qualities and influences you need that day and letting God's great plan of good for your life reveal and express itself that day through you. Eternal life is meant to be lived daily.

As you awaken each day, know that today is ripe with opportunities for you to have a God-filled day, a spiritually successful day of learning and growing and becoming more of what God created you to be. Then, lift up your eyes; become alert and aware of the good at hand. See what life brings to you this day and look at it with the eyes of Spirit. Then, see what you can bring to life in this day. Know that even problems, hardships, and tragedies can be met and overcome one day at a time in a way that can change your life. Each day learn to make the best of all that comes and the least of all that goes.

Remember, creative experiences are cumulative, and any experience well-lived today will bring new opportunities and open up new possibilities that will lead you higher and higher in expressing your spiritual potential.

God's plan for you is unique. Yet, all of us are meant to live and enjoy our lives as daily adventures—to live out today's good as it comes in whatever form. Learn to enjoy the ecstasy of God's Spirit in you expressing itself in the midst of your everyday life experiences. Life is full of spiritual possibilities—each day holds unexpected treasures, new thoughts, new insights, new dreams, new joys, and new creative opportunities. Each encounter brings the potential of spiritual vision.

Lift up your eyes and you will discover that every day offers precious moments in which we can experience the presence of God. Learn to live in the joy, the beauty, and the glory that can be found within these priceless eternal moments and you will discover that you have tapped the source of all creation and that you are indeed living in the mainstream and on the crest of the wave of God's magnificent creative process.

Then you will have all the power you will ever need for every good thing in your life. The secret can be easily remembered in the prayer of an old Scotsman, *"Lord, teach me to live every day of my life!"*

Meanwhile, Back at the Kingdom

Shakespeare said: *There's a divinity that shapes our ends.* It's true. There is a higher power in each of us—Spirit. We are entering an age of Spirit. It will be very new to us in many ways—with surprising new dimensions of experience.

This mysterious and dramatic new era now being born will push out all the boundaries of the world as we now know it. It will literally change the face of the Earth and usher in an entirely new life. Yet, that which is being born is born of Spirit, and the real activity and the greatest drama will occur within each of us, brought forth and sent forth from the silent center of our own indwelling spiritual potential.

Jesus came to introduce us to this spiritual side of life hidden within ourselves: the kingdom of God or the kingdom of heaven, as He called it. But He knew that spiritual things must be spiritually discerned. So, in presenting His teachings, He avoided the static limits of creed, doctrines, and dogmas, and used instead simple, commonplace stories. These stories are able to convey His eternal lessons of spiritual Truth to everyone throughout the ages—as each one becomes ready for them. I believe that if He were physically among us now, He might use our interest in sports for illustrations of spiritual Truth.

Joe Namath, one of the best quarterbacks in football history, once told how he was transformed from a good to a great quarterback in a single moment. As do all athletes, he practiced and trained for years, both physically and mentally, in his football skills. Then, one day as he was calling signals for a play, he was suddenly able to "read" the defense. And, in his words, for the first time: *"the heavens opened up."* From that time on, "Broadway Joe" had a different level of awareness than the ordinary football player.

Jesus came to open up the heavens for us—literally. This lesson is about that—the experience we now call rebirth—being born again in Spirit. And, as Jesus said, it is for those who have *"ears to hear."* So, right now let's switch off all the loaves and fishes (our interests and concerns) that command most of our attention and let Jesus' teaching take us beyond the narrow confines of our ordinary, earthbound, and mundane lives and introduce us to the larger life that awaits us: that eternal life of spiritual consciousness and spiritual living.

The story is about Nicodemus.

Now there was a man of the Pharisees, named Nicodemus, a ruler of the Jews. This man came to Jesus by night and said to him, "Rabbi, we know that you are a teacher come from God; for no one

*can do these signs that you do, unless God is with
him." Jesus answered him, "Truly, truly, I say to
you, unless one is born anew, he cannot see the
kingdom of God." Nicodemus said to him, "How
can a man be born when he is old? Can he enter a
second time into his mother's womb and be
born?" Jesus answered, "Truly, truly, I say to you,
unless one is born of water and the Spirit, he cannot enter into the kingdom of God. That which is
born of the flesh is flesh, and that which is born of
the Spirit is spirit. Do not marvel that I said to you,
'You must be born anew.' The wind blows where
it wills, and you hear the sound of it, but you do
not know whence it comes or whither it goes; so it
is with every one who is born of the Spirit."* (John
3:1-8)

Jesus gave two of His greatest sermons to an
audience of one person each. One was to the
woman at the well and the other to Nicodemus.
The woman represents the "bottom of the pile" of
human life. Nicodemus represents the "top of the
heap."

Nicodemus was a Pharisee, meaning that he
was a VIP in every way that meant anything to a
Jew, and to most human beings. He was educated, rich, probably young—a leader in his country's government and religion and social life. He
was probably one of the few people who didn't
originally approach Jesus for the "loaves and

fishes"—he didn't need anything that the world could give. But, with everything he did have, including his religion, there was still something lacking in his life. Probably intuitively he recognized that Jesus had the answer.

He came to Jesus by night, embarrassed to be seen, and asked Jesus to explain the kingdom He had been teaching about. Jesus used this opportunity to make it clear in the very beginning that all intellectual inquiries about the kingdom are to no avail. It is a spiritual kingdom, which can only be comprehended and entered into by those who are spiritually quickened or, in Jesus' words, *"born anew." [born again]* (A.V.)

Nicodemus then asked what might seem to us a rather absurd question for a man of his intelligence: *"How can a man be born when he is old? Can he enter a second time into his mother's womb and be born?* We usually assume that the answer is obviously "no." But Jesus didn't indicate that it was a silly question, because the answer, I believe, is really yes. For spiritual growth we do need to enter again our mother's womb and be born again in our imagination.

Follow this through in your thinking. In Genesis, which means the book of beginnings, we read that God created us in His image and likeness and pronounced us good. In other words, God created us out of His own creative Spirit, with his spiritual Nature, to be coexpressers with Him in His creation. Jesus' message is that the spiritual seed of God is planted in us (the kingdom of heaven) and the key to eternal life (the fullness of expressing God's indwelling Nature in us) is knowing that we *are* children of God and heirs to His all good Nature.

In the story of Nicodemus, Jesus gives us the secret of spiritual living; He takes us back to our spiritual origin. He is saying, in effect, "Enter again in your imagination into your mother's womb—that time before your human physical birthday, back to that initial moment when you became flesh—one little living cell." Then ask yourself, "Is that the beginning of me?" And you will see that it isn't at all!

Flesh can only beget flesh. The beginning you had in your mother was only for this life on Earth. Spirit begets spirit. Your original birth was when you were created in the spiritual image and likeness of God. This knowledge is the starting point for real spiritual attainment—establishing yourself in this spiritual Truth about yourself as well as God.

Jesus is teaching a higher order of truth than Nicodemus ever knew in his religion, or is yet understood in most religions even today. He is disclosing an entirely new perspective that requires a new way of thinking. Jesus is revealing the spiritual Truth about the possibilities of an inner evolution from our so-called "natural" (human) way of life into our spiritual potential. He is disclosing how we can awaken to and be born again and again from that selfsame creative Spirit that has brought us this far and can move us ever upward and onward into newer, higher levels beyond our present selves.

" . . . *unless one is born anew* . . . " he cannot see the possibilities of the expanding potential of his own spiritual nature. This great sermon on rebirth was the core-essence and the real meaning of all that Jesus taught. But Nicodemus was too attached, too satisfied with his somewhat privileged life and his orthodox way of thinking to immediately take on new priorities and new loyalties and open the way to an altogether new life. He "knew not what spirit he was of." The conversation with Nicodemus therefore became a turning point in Jesus' ministry, for Nicodemus represents the general attitude of the people in Jerusalem. They were bound to the old, traditional beliefs, quite satisfied with them, and too closed-minded and defensive to learn from Jesus. As a result, Jesus decided to leave Jerusalem and go to Galilee where people were less educated and sophisticated but more open and receptive to something new.

The unregenerated person who doesn't know

what spirit he is of, no matter how intelligent or successful in a worldly way, can only muddle through until the time that he is born of Spirit and awakened to his spiritual possibilities.

The real purpose of all human life is the growth and unfoldment of our spiritual potential through spiritualized living. Nicodemus wasn't quite ready. But I believe by virtue of your having been drawn to a new age religion—a religion of Spirit and Truth such as Unity—the Spirit in you, the Lord of your being, having guided you all along from your original spiritual conception of God's image to the present time, knows that now you are ready to enter the consciousness of spiritual living. In fact, you probably already have.

But, at this special time of accelerated change, I think we need to be reminded that the process of birth (both physical and spiritual), which is one of the greatest miracles and joys in all life, is also a time of pain and confusion. It isn't easy to let go of a familiar world, even though the new one is full of promise. If you are going through confusion and some unusual and surprising changes, take heart! This is the transition period. We are in the midst of a great spiritual upliftment—a cosmic quantum leap—the birth of a new age of spiritual living.

What should you do? Cooperate! Make rebirth a daily experience in your life. Make it top priority in your life to become increasingly aware of God's presence. Become God-oriented. Learn to look for God's spiritual influence in all the ways it does work in your life; that is, the spiritual meaning behind anything that is going on in your life. And over and over learn to practice the truth of your own being related to everything you do. Claim the consciousness of the mind that was in Christ Jesus that will put you in touch with your own spiritual nature and begin to open the heavens of your own spiritual potential.

Prayer and meditation are the basic exercises of Spirit—you won't get far without them, and you shouldn't want to. Taking the time each day to go apart a while in prayer and meditation ought to become as important and enjoyable to you as the meals you eat. But also, besides these special times, we need to cultivate a continuing sense of spiritual awareness that is in operation in even the most active times of our day.

Do you know the story about the farmer and the cricket in New York City? On the sidewalk of busy, noisy Fifth Avenue, a city dweller saw a man standing with his ear cupped—apparently listening to something. He asked him about it, and the man said that he was listening to a cricket. The city dweller said he had never heard a cricket in New York City. The man said, "I'll show you why." He took a coin out of his pocket and tossed it in the air and it fell on the sidewalk. It wasn't very loud, but suddenly for half a block on either side, everybody stopped and looked around. He then explained that he was a farmer and that his ears were tuned to crickets. He concluded: "We all hear what we're tuned to."

I have a Unity friend in Wichita, a very successful and practical banker, who once told me that his highest goal in life was to achieve a state of consciousness in which every moment of his life, in whatever he was doing, he had in the background of his mind at least a vague awareness of the presence of God. He obviously practiced his aspiration, for it was an inspiration and a pleasure to be in his company.

As with the farmer in New York and my friend in Wichita, we need to cultivate a higher sensitivity. We need to practice being spiritually centered so that we increasingly become spiritually oriented and spirit-minded. We need "GIHR"—*God Is Here Reminders*.

The lesson we learn from the story of Nicodemus is to actually *practice* being "born again." Do you really want to improve your life, to become whole, healthy, and successful in the right way? Get vitally interested in life and live it to the hilt! But train yourself also to stop often throughout the busy involvement of your day for brief retreats into the silence of the inner kingdom. Take short spiritual pauses in which you return, in your thoughts and feelings, to your spiritual origins and are reminded of the truth of your being and renewed in its image.

You are a spiritual being. There is so much more in you than you now know about, or have ever been told, or could even believe if someone could find the words to tell you. But Jesus summed it all up by saying, " . . . *the kingdom of God is in the midst of you.*" (Luke 17:20) He also said that the kingdom comes not with observation, but by getting busy and being about our Father's business.

He added that: " . . . *the wind blows where it wills . . . *"—the kingdom of heaven in you will open up in its own good time. The word "heaven" means expansion—expanding potential. It never comes full-blown or all at once. But each new birth brings forth more potential and each stage of growth increases the leaven.

Heaven most often comes to us in little moments, little insights in which the infinite glories of God light up our commonplace view of life, little breakthroughs of inspiration, forgiveness, peace, understanding, joy, and love, little disclosures of our own indwelling divinity. Each disclosure will add the powerful leaven of spirit to our lives, lifting us into new lives and a new world, by creating out of us surprising new persons. This is the great intrigue in life, the great adventure, the great miracle, . . . *the mystery hidden for ages . . . Christ in you, the hope of glory.* (Col. 1:26, 27)

Your hidden potential is with you always. It eternally dwells in you. Learn, in whatever you are involved with in the enterprise of living your life, to be aware of and take into account the spiritual resource that is ever waiting to be born into your life. It is always your greatest asset!

The Lamb of God

This Bible drama introduces us to a colorful and fascinating biblical character, John the Baptist. We remember him as one who came out of the wilderness, wearing rough clothing, disdaining material things, denouncing worldly powers and, in harsh language, sternly warning everyone to *"Repent,"* or else! And yet, John the Baptist is also the one who introduced us to Jesus with the gentle dove-like words, . . . *"Behold, the Lamb of God, who takes away the sin of the world!"* (John 1:29)

John the Baptist, of course, represents something very important in our own spiritual development. John was the forerunner of Jesus. In us, he symbolizes the intellectual perception of spiritual things that prepares for the advent of spiritualized consciousness. Jesus said about John: *"This is he of whom it is written, 'Behold, I send my messenger before thy face, who shall prepare thy way before thee.' Truly, I say to you, among those born of women there has risen no one greater than John the Baptist; yet he who is least in the kingdom of heaven is greater than he."* (Matt. 11:10)

John, in his illuminated awareness, said about Jesus: *"He must increase, but I must decrease."* (John 4:30) One of the greatest achievements of our intellect is the realization that it must give way to higher spiritual understanding and that even the least perception of spiritually quickened thought is greater than the mightiest achievements of the human intellect.

John the Baptist symbolizes in each individual the "natural man" who has begun to recognize the innate higher spiritual nature—the intellect, which has turned toward the light. He typifies the intellectual consciousness that has begun to think about things on a higher level than just facts, theories, or opinions. He has glimpsed what he knows to be a higher Truth and he readily pays homage to it. But John still strives with evil as a reality. He has an intellectual perception of Truth, but he is not yet quickened by Spirit.

The John the Baptist level of consciousness continues to work almost entirely under that law given by Moses—the operation of cause and effect that helps guide and correct us within the provision of definite boundaries and limitations. Grace and Truth, which came through Jesus, lead past the limits of the "natural man" into a higher working of law, which fulfills all things in love.

The *"Lamb of God"* is a wonderful symbol of the love activity seen so beautifully in the person of Jesus. The blood of the Lamb is emblematic of the liberalizing, uplifting, perfecting quality of God's love in action. (To the ancient Hebrews a "lamb" represented innocent, guileless harmlessness. "Blood" was thought to be the actual form of Spirit).

When John looked at Jesus and announced: *"Behold, the Lamb of God, who takes away the sin of the world,"* he was introducing us to one of the most benevolent qualities of God's creation, the *forgiving love of Jesus Christ*—the love of a pure heart that takes away all sins and washes them clean. John was dramatically introducing us to the ever-present love of the living Christ that offers us continuous forgiveness of all our sins.

Forgiveness is immensely important. To some degree the activity of forgiveness is constantly at work—healing, dissolving, helping overcome the mistakes, hurts, and vexations of life. But still, many things remain unforgiven in each of us, and there is nothing that holds us back in life and in our spiritual progress more than a state of unforgiveness.

Much of our unforgiveness is about ourselves. We all live with some continuing sense of self-condemnation and punishment about anything for which we haven't forgiven ourselves. This often gives us a poor self-image. Unforgiveness of ourselves blocks us—often completely stifles us—from expressing our own best qualities. This deprives us of the things we want and need most in life, and often makes us our own worst enemy.

Unforgiveness of others is equally devastating to us. When we hold unforgiving feelings about others, we build a shell around ourselves and arrest ourselves at that level. We are imprisoned by our own unforgiveness and are unable to rise above the caliber of our own thoughts and emotions. Unforgiveness is always supported and maintained entirely by negative, destructive, and poisonous thoughts and feelings no matter how justified it may seem.

The unforgiving person is always stymied and restricted to the narrow, unpleasant, binding memories of the past and unable to give and participate fully and freely in the present. Yet, it is almost "magic" that each time we experience forgiveness about anything we immediately open ourselves to a more creative, constructive, and productive life.

Few experiences can exceed the feelings of freedom, joy, and love that follow a simple action of forgiveness for ourselves or someone else. Forgiveness is always a transforming activity. First of all, it is a release from the prisons of the past. Secondly, it is a breakthrough into new possibilities for the future. And third, it is an activation of new forces for good that go to work in our lives.

In an army barracks, a tough cynical soldier from the city badgered a young, naive country boy at every chance. One night, the youth from the country kneeled down beside his bunk to pray, and his antagonist hurled a muddy boot that hit him so hard it stunned him. The next morning, the boot-throwing soldier reached for his muddy boots and found them cleaned and polished. It changed everything. The two soldiers became friends, and the entire company was brought closer together with new respect and true esprit de corps.

Forgiveness always releases us from some kind of bondage, puts us more in control, and lifts us into new possibilities. It is not easy, intellectually, to forgive. At times it seems almost impossible. Even with the high intellectual perception of John the Baptist there are serious limits to our ability to truly forgive ourselves and others. We really just don't seem to have the ability to out-think negativity on an intellectual level. We need help.

Baptism is a symbol of purification. John's type of baptism, symbolized by water, is the first step in cleaning our minds of deeply held mistakes and errors. It is the step that prepares us to receive the cleansing that can take place by the all-powerful Spirit in us. Jesus baptized with the Holy Spirit, the ultimate purification of the blood of the Lamb.

The intellectual baptism of John, by water purification, can be compared with what we in Unity call denial. The mental activity of repenting means changing our minds about our beliefs that are not

181

in tune with spiritual Truth. Denial convinces us intellectually that something isn't true. We couple this with affirmations that support new beliefs based on the spiritual possibilities that can be brought forth. The work is done in consciousness—mentally and spiritually. We prepare our minds and hearts for something higher—God provides the increase.

Charles Fillmore advised that forgiveness really means giving up something. We give up the lesser for the greater. We give up resentments, condemnations, and overly immature sensitive feelings and replace them with greater, more ennobling kinds of thoughts and feelings. It is, however, the activity of Spirit that does the real work. By cultivating our higher thoughts and feelings represented by John the Baptist, we remove some of the obstacles, and then Spirit can become an active factor in our consciousness.

Perhaps from an intellectual point of view we can think about forgiveness as a "point of agreement" between two mature and loving parents who settle an argument between children. Establish that kind of mental control in your inner life and you automatically open yourself to greater understanding, tolerance, humor, good will; and you will considerably brighten your life.

One of the most beautiful and memorable qualities in Jesus' life was His forgiveness. He forgave everyone. Truly, He was the Lamb of God—the loving forgiveness that takes away the sin of the world. The loving forgiveness of Jesus Christ is one of God's greatest gifts to each of us. It can clean and purify any part or level of our consciousness, removing deep hurts, grudges, resentments, painful memories, and even wrongs that have never happened. It can flood our minds and hearts with a powerful spiritual medicine that purifies and heals everything that holds us back from spiritual growth. The blood of the Lamb is one of the most precious qualities of the Christ of God. It is one of the most precious truths you can know about.

God's love and its healing qualities can redeem anything in us. It is constantly available, but it needs to be accepted. It needs our attention and acceptance now. There are many things in life and spiritual growth that require patience. But forgiveness is always a "now" thing; it is not something to put off.

Two of England's greatest authors, Charles Dickens and William Thackery, developed a rivalry and finally a bitter animosity toward each other. Eventually they met and at first refused to recognize each other. But Thackery suddenly turned back and grasped Dicken's hand. He told him that he could no longer bear the coldness between them and the old jealousy was dissolved on the spot. Almost immediately afterward, Thackery died suddenly. Dickens said that one of the deepest joys in his life was that he had accepted his friend's warm handshake before the opportunity had been lost forever.

In Revelation 7:14 is the promise: We can wash our robes—our human garments, our personalities—and have them made *white in the blood of the Lamb.* We can be led into the fountain of living water which will wipe the tears from our eyes!

Tapping the Source

I have always been intrigued with the notion that a simple, everyday incident can change a person's entire life. Jesus once had an apparently insignificant conversation with a seemingly undistinguished person in what was considered an unimportant locale, but which probably unveiled one of the most enlightening, yet overlooked, spiritual revelations in the Bible. The unpretentious incident dramatized a major overview of Jesus' teachings—the idea that God is Spirit. This is the foundation concept of Unity's interpretation of Jesus' teaching: that God is the universal Father of creation, whose infinite presence or *"kingdom"* as Jesus said, is always *"at hand,"* within.

In this chapter we are going to take a deeper look at the omnipresent reservoir of God's tremendous spiritual resources that reside within each of us, by joining Jesus at the Samaritan well—a story told in the Gospel of John. Jesus had begun his ministry in and around Jerusalem, the center of the Jewish religion. From the conversation Jesus had with Nicodemus, we learned that the people of Jerusalem were too proud and too bound to tradition to accept anything new. So Jesus made a decision to take His ministry north to Galilee, where the people were less educated and sophisticated but were more receptive and teachable.

To take up the story, Jesus left Jerusalem and set out for Galilee. Between Jerusalem and Galilee was Samaria. A very revealing line in the story says: *He (Jesus) had to pass through Samaria.* (John 4:4) The Jews of Judea considered themselves the spiritual aristocracy and they despised the Samaritans, whom they considered a mixed breed. No self-respecting Jew would set foot in Samaria. Therefore, Jesus' arrival in Samaria is, in itself, an important teaching. And there, as He stopped for a drink of water at a well, He met the woman. The seemingly incidental conversation between Jesus and the woman is truly one of the most important stories in the Bible.

It was the sixth hour, which meant noon in that day. This reveals much about the life and the problems of this woman. The significance of the time is that she is getting her daily supply of water at the hottest time of the day. Why? It was probably to avoid all the other women of the village. She was an outcast, a so-called "sinful" woman with a "past." After having asked for a drink of literal water, Jesus almost immediately introduced the subject of spiritual water—a "living water" from which one need never thirst again. Then, from this exalted scale of meaning, He descended into what seems to be a very commonplace moral criticism of the woman by pointing out to her that she has had five husbands and isn't even married to her present companion. Actually, Jesus had a very tender regard for women and was always respectful and sympathetic to them. But, as He often did, Jesus used this fact as a stepping-stone to something higher. In Bible symbology, "women" represent our emotions, or our feeling nature. (Men represent the intellect.) In this story, the "five husbands" represent the avenues of knowledge and awareness of our five senses. The "woman at the well" represents the deep emotional longings we all have for something in our lives that will truly satisfy the spiritual needs of our souls. The various relationships she had had with different men refer to the diverging inner unions that can take place between our thoughts and feelings.

This story is about the kind of union that takes place in our thoughts and feelings when our emotions and our deep spiritual longings are dominated by the limited intellectual understanding that comes from our five senses alone. This union is always a spiritually unfulfilling and unsuccessful "marriage" of the inner life. These five husbands are all wrong unions in which our emotions and basic drives receive inadequate support and fail to get the true understanding.

The sixth outright unmarried relationship

means no union at all with truth—a complete rejection of anything about our spiritual nature.

The well in the story is a beautiful symbol of deep prayer and meditation. Jesus is telling us about learning to draw from the spiritual side of our nature—to add the spiritual increase to our five-senses-understanding through inspiration and intuition. He is introducing us to a "living water," a living spiritual influence that can quicken our latent resources, make us more alive from within ourselves, and lead us into soul growth and higher development. The story teaches us that the foundation of life is the omnipresent Spirit of God in us, and it reveals the truth about how we can inaugurate changes from the higher realms within ourselves and enter into larger life. The dramatic change in the Samaritan woman reveals an aliveness that draws directly from the inner fount of those riches of God by which our spiritual nature comes into its own and truly satisfies all the longings of our thirsty souls. These are the everlasting qualities that endure long after the treasures of the world rust, tarnish, fade, and are gone with the wind—leaving us to thirst again.

The whole story of the Samaritan well is about a special kind of truth that concerns the possibility of our individual change and growth from the power of the latent spirit within us. Jesus is telling us through the woman at the well that we can't draw the qualities of eternal life out of the old cisterns of our strictly human selves. We can't invent or image a new being for ourselves out of what we know or can receive from our five senses alone. But, if we knew the gift of God—the power of His nature and potential in us—we could then open ourselves to the flow of the living water of God's life, love, intelligence, and substance that flows from the Source—the indwelling Fountainhead, God. Jesus is saying, if we will ask the Source for any real or good thing, we will get it.

As a girl, Myrtle Fillmore had a dream that she later remembered in connection with her life-changing healing that gave birth to the Unity movement. This dream was a beautiful vision about the fount of the living spirit within. I quote from Thomas E. Witherspoon's book, *Myrtle Fillmore: Mother of Unity:*

> "There was a bed of a stream that must have been active at some time. It was beautiful, with white, sandy bottom, but all the water it held was in a few bowls of white rock—apparently a dried-up stream. Stopping to investigate, I could find no source. A very high ledge of rock crossed its bed at the south, and looking to the north I could see only a continuous bed of like character as that before me. In my astonishment, I voiced the question, 'From whence the source of this

stream?' And for answer there came a sudden voice, more of waters than anything else, 'I will show you.' And over the ledge of rock came pouring a regular Niagara. I had to get back further into the woods, away from the spray. It ceased when the bed was filled. As I stood looking at the clear water of the stream, beautiful flowers sprang up. This is one of my many dreams, the meaning of which was to be made plain afterwards, although at the time Scripture verses came to me about the rock of salvation and the waters of life. When my life stream was low, and I was about to lose it, and then there came pouring into me this truth, I saw more clearly the meaning of the dream. I remembered the source of my life (where the source of my life was and how it came over the rock that was higher than I). Where there had seemed to be lack and low pressure of life, there was now free-flowing more abundant Christ life, made fruitful unto good works through His power, wisdom, and love."

As we return to the Bible story, we find Jesus telling the woman about worshiping in spirit and truth. She then tells him that, as do the Jews, she believes in the Messiah. And with this, for the first time to anyone, Jesus told her straight out: *"I who speak to you am he."* (John 4:26) She was so overcome and transformed that years of shame, bitterness, and feelings of unworthiness were instantly washed away by this living water. She ran through the streets shouting to everyone, *"Come, see a man who told me all that I ever did. Can this be the Christ?"* (John 4:29) Many of the Samaritans believed and wanted Him to stay; but in a few days, He had to move on.

Worship means worth-ship: to value, to esteem, to identify, to experience personally. A seeming chance encounter with Christ spiritually impelled almost a whole town into a glorious new consciousness.

Think of the miraculous change in this one woman who, up to this time, only wanted to draw some literal water from the town well without having to face anyone in her shame. She soared from the ridiculous to the sublime, from the mundane to the universal. Think also of her fellow Samaritans, whose greatest asset may have been their lack of religious and cultural bonds, and who, therefore, could readily recognize and eagerly respond to the Christ and become radiantly alive!

Each of us now lives only a fraction of that larger life that we can call forth from the well of Spirit in our own being. Jesus' message is the message of Unity—there is but one Source of being. This Source is the omnipresent, living fountain—all good—be it life, love, wisdom, or power. This Source and you are connected every moment of your existence. You have the ability to draw on this Source for all the good you will ever need or ever be capable of desiring. Only the expression of those everlasting qualities of your own spiritual nature will ever satisfy you.

Mary or Martha, Which?

From the biblical story of Martha and Mary we can learn an all-important truth about how to let all the spiritual potentials in us have greater expression with the least amount of human interference.

Martha, Mary, and their brother Lazarus lived in the small village of Bethany just outside Jerusalem. They were especially close friends with Jesus. Jesus hadn't made many intimate friends during his ministry, and only a few persons understood Him. But this one home where His three good friends lived was a place that He loved to go.

There is evidence that this was a family of means, and that they gave of their means, as well as of themselves. Mary, for example, used her costly ointment on Jesus. Their home undoubtedly was very comfortable and inviting. Martha and Mary, however, were as different in temperament and in their approaches to spiritual awareness as two people could be. Martha was likely the older. She was practical, active, and solid. She excelled as a "homemaker" and strove for perfection around the house. She always took the lead and probably "mothered" Mary.

Mary was more pensive, quiet yet imaginative, sensitive, and spiritually impassioned. Though their natures were poles apart, they were closely bound, and Jesus understood and loved them both.

It is at an increasingly difficult time in Jesus' life that the Bible introduces us to Martha and Mary. Jesus was constantly facing mounting opposition and the Cross. It was at this favored house in Bethany, blessed with peace, faith, and love, that He could pause for a brief while and rest with His friends. Here is where we see the contrast in Martha and Mary. Martha immediately began to hustle and bustle, making preparations for an elaborate feast worthy of Jesus and doing everything to make Him comfortable and to honor His presence in their home.

In trying to do the best she could, she fussed, worried, and got herself into a tizzy. Mary, on the other hand, sat at Jesus' feet in a quiet spiritual rapture, drinking in every word, eager to learn the lessons He had to teach. There is nothing really wrong with either attitude; both reflect loving concern. But Martha thought something was wrong because Mary wasn't helping her at all during this rush period. She complained to Jesus: *"Lord, do you not care that my sister has left me to serve alone? Tell her then to help me."* (Luke 10:40) I'm sure most housewives would tend to sympathize with Martha.

But Jesus didn't. He corrected Martha, not

198

Mary. He said to her: *"Martha, Martha, you are anxious and troubled about many things; one thing is needful. Mary has chosen the good portion, which shall not be taken away from her."* (Luke 10:41)

Martha's shortcoming, besides resenting and grumbling, was a mistaken emphasis. Martha's activities and service were good but going in the wrong direction. She was hustling, bustling, and becoming tense and anxious when Jesus very much wanted only peace, quiet, and spiritual support. She was preparing a lavish feast when at the moment He wanted only a simple meal. He had only one great need—food for the soul. Mary had that one thing. Through her loving attention to Jesus, she showed evidence of knowing not only His needs but probably more of the secrets of His truth and power and wisdom than even His disciples did. Because of this, she was undoubtedly one of the most spiritually sensitive people in all of Jesus' life. It would have been far more important for Martha at that time to have ceased her busy work for Jesus and listen to Him that she might serve Him far better. Martha's kind of work makes us tired, exhausted, and it depletes the energies of mind and body. Prayer infills us spiritually; it expands and strengthens the powers of our souls.

It is fairly common for new Unity students, where prayer is emphasized so strongly, to wonder about the place of active work in their religious outlook. Unity leaves it strictly to each individual as to what he or she does and how to use Truth. But it isn't that we spend all our time in prayer and sit back and never do anything. Good Unity students are constantly "about their Father's business."

The principle involved is contained in an old Quaker saying: "Pray and then move your feet." It means, of course, pray first and then take appropriate action. Martha and Mary, you remember, were sisters. They were very closely related. Prayer and effective outer activity are also closely related. They too are sisters.

There is a divine order for getting things done. Jesus firmly instructed us to seek first the kingdom. Prayer comes first, and right action follows; otherwise, our activities take over and lead us astray. The contemplative, thoughtful, listening, and receptive way of Mary must ever predominate and provide its elevating, uplifting, and guiding influence. One thing is needful—devotion to the Christ.

A teacher once said to a third-grader: "What keeps you from getting your homework done?" With remarkable understanding, the youngster said: "Just me." There are all kinds of busy thoughts and feelings that go through our minds and emotions. Our inner world gets overcrowded;

it is hard for a new idea to get in and even more difficult for the "still small voice" to be heard. That was the problem with the way of Martha. She was so preoccupied with "trifles" and arrangements that she didn't even have time to listen to Jesus Christ Himself!

We have to learn to eliminate non-essentials— not to be so "... *troubled about many things."* (Luke 10:41) To take matters into our own hands is to delay the answer. That is why Jesus said that Mary had chosen the better part. Her interest in spiritual values kept her absorbed in more important matters. She was open and receptive to the treasures of Spirit. Learning Truth, gaining spiritual insight, and preparing her inner life so that the Spirit could work remarkable transformations in her life made Mary capable of more effective service. Jesus loved and respected Martha, but He treated Mary as a full-fledged disciple.

As we can learn from the third-grader, the thing that hinders our spiritual growth is just us. Those who are always anxiously working with human concerns cannot pray effectively or keep their attention focused on the ultimate spiritual purposes of life.

Conversely, those who withdraw entirely into prayer and contemplation never fulfill their God-given spiritual potentials either. The ideal person is a balanced combination of the traits of Martha and Mary—receptive and inspired first, which saves us a lot of anxiety, wasted time, and effort. Then we are able to go ahead as a working channel through which God can work out His great plans and purposes, using all our human talents and abilities.

In Unity our approach is what Charles Fillmore called "practical mysticism"—we study and pray, establishing truth, order, peace, faith, and love in our inner world; then we "move our feet," reinforced by the Father within who does the works. This is an unfailing way to bring God into our lives, to live out our highest concept of what is Christlike, and to become partners with God in the creation of ourselves.

Strange Brotherhood

In this chapter we find another unforgettable drama that Jesus wove into the tapestry of His teaching. We have already identified the central theme of His teaching as something that has come to be known in English as the "kingdom"—the kingdom of God, or the kingdom of heaven, which we believe is the infinite, omnipresent spiritual realm that is behind, beyond, and within all creation.

We have also explored Jesus' kingdom message from several viewpoints, especially from the emphasis of His own words that the kingdom is *"at hand"* and *"in the midst of you."* The truth that we have recognized in His words about this is that, as God's spiritual image and likeness, each of us has—ever available and accessible within ourselves—an indwelling kingdom of God's inherent spiritual potentials and possibilities that can be quickened and brought forth into our lives through our own minds and hearts.

We have further seen that, by not having understood this truth about ourselves, most of our lives are lived exactly backward, in that we strive with the futility of dealing with the endless situations and circumstances of outward effects rather than establishing dominion and authority in the inner domain of causes. In other words, most of the time we cope and contend—and rarely do we really live!

Jesus constantly redirected us within, to the realm of spiritual causation, from which we can inwardly invoke God's universal creative process in our own consciousness and, thereby, outwardly into our lives and world.

This connotes that the formative work of a life dedicated to the way, the truth, and the life of Jesus Christ is done *within,* by the discipleship of our thoughts and feelings, and the awakening to our latent spiritual potentials through study, prayer, and meditation. Jesus established both the priorities and order of the Christ life with His precept: *"But seek first his kingdom and his righteousness [right-thinking], and all these things shall be yours as well."* (Matt. 6:33)

The great news of Jesus' message is that each of us carries the kingdom of God's nature and His infinite, creative potential within at all times. It is our indwelling legacy from our heavenly Father. And, like the prodigal son, as soon as we turn to Him, our heritage becomes an active reality in our lives. We are born into a new dimension of living and enter into a creative partnership with our Father that brings forth a life of growth, mastery, and spiritual power—the kind of life we were designed to live—the kind of life that was lived by our Elder Brother, Jesus Christ.

It is vital to understand that the creative process by which life is successfully lived is always established and initiated within. But, once it is quickened within, it is equally important to provide a channel for its outward expression.

Let us now look at one of the great Bible dramas that can teach us how to translate spiritual Truth into action and bring our inner potential forth as force for good in our lives. The drama is Jesus' parable of the Good Samaritan.

The story starts with a conversation between Jesus and a Jewish lawyer. A "lawyer" at that time didn't mean a member of the legal profession but a student and expounder of the religious laws of Israel. As with the scribes, they represented the lifeless, mechanical, legalistic attitude of obeying the *letter* of the law rather than developing the potential benefits of pursuing the *spirit* of the law.

In this situation, the lawyer had asked Jesus a question: *". . . Teacher, what shall I do to inherit eternal life?"* (Luke 10:25) It is significant to know that this occurred during the last six months of Jesus' ministry, when the religious hierarchy was becoming increasingly hostile toward Jesus. The lawyer may have been a "plant" attempting to argue with Jesus in order to trip Him up and launch an attack. On the other hand, this represents a very natural question that might be asked by any sincere religious seeker. So, let's give the lawyer the benefit of the doubt. Let's say that he had sensed, as many do, that there is a much greater possibility to life than we have yet realized—an eternal quality that has nothing to do with the mere passage of time or what happens to us after we die but is a magnificent potential that can take us beyond anything we now experience into new, richer, fuller dimensions of "life more abundant." The lawyer might have been saying, especially in the presence of Jesus Christ: "I can glimpse something of what you mean by this larger 'Eternal' life. But how do I come into it?" Jesus may have replied to the lawyer's question: "You ought to know the answer yourself, as a lawyer. What is written in the law about this?" The lawyer answered: "Well, the law is 'Love the Lord your God with all your soul and all your strength and all your mind." And Jesus said something like: "That's it!" Do that and you shall live."

But do what? How do you love that way?

To love God, we must know God—and know the right things about Him. There are many, many good and wonderful things to know about God. It is especially important to know that "God is love," and to know how He loves us.

In this story of the Good Samaritan, Jesus gave us a memorable, dramatic example of an incident of God-like love in the life of a human being. In the story, an unfortunate traveler became a victim of roadway thieves. He was beaten and stripped of his possessions, which included his clothes, and left lying half dead in a ditch beside the road.

By coincidence, a priest came by. He saw the body and immediately passed by on the other side of the road. One thing that we might remember on his behalf is that a priest was never to touch a dead body or he would be unclean for his priestly duties for the next twenty-four hours. Also, most devoted men of his day regarded all suffering as decreed by God. Why should they concern themselves or try to interfere with an "act of God"? Clearly, however, the priest put his ecclesiastical duties before an act of kindness or an opportunity to express the law of love.

After the priest passed by, a Levite came, perhaps thinking, "If the priest leaves him alone, why should I bother with him?"

Then, the nonreligious person came along, a Samaritan on a business journey. When he saw the man in trouble, he crossed the road—to help! Very compassionately, he poured oil and wine on the wounds, bound the man up (medically speaking), placed him on his own donkey, and took him to the inn. There is then the wonderful suggestion that he watched over the hapless stranger all night, and in the morning he made generous arrangement for extended care.

When Jesus finished His story, He asked the lawyer, in effect, "Who then, of these three, was the neighbor?" The Jews had such a loathing and contempt for the Samaritans that the lawyer wouldn't even mention the word in answering the question. He replied, "Oh, well, the neighbor is the one who had mercy." Jesus concluded, *"Go and do likewise."* (Luke 10:37) Go and put that kind of love into action, and you will know a new dimension of life.

The answer to, "Who is my neighbor?" according to Jesus, is *anyone who needs my help!* To the Jew, this was a startling departure from his religious views. He did feel a definite responsibility to his fellow Jews, but none at all to Gentiles.

An act of love and kindness has its birth in feelings of mutual respect and caring. One of England's prime ministers, in need of an operation, informed the doctor, "I don't want you to treat me as though I were one of the poor charity wretches that come to your hospital." "Sir, you would be very fortunate if I did; for these poor, miserable charity wretches (as you call them) are all prime ministers in my eyes!"

God's love is poured out fully on all His children. The notion of "favorites" is a human misconception. God's love, transformed into our love for another, must see them as loved by God, and, therefore, our neighbors—our brother and sister.

Remember, this parable was told by Jesus who loved each of us that way! Accepting His approach as our own is a marvelous new chance to break through a lot of barriers and experience a new quality to our lives that we have never known before.

There are many reasons why we withhold our love from others. None of them is worth it. They are all negatives—fear, anger, resentment, jealousy, or envy. They not only cause us to ration our love to others but quickly inhibit our ability to experience what love can add to our lives. Sentiment is also a weak basis for love. It depends on emotions that are often capricious and even sloshy and can suddenly change or evaporate. True compassion runs much deeper.

What we need is the overcoming strength of a more-than-human power, namely the love of God. So often we feel we must change someone in order that we can love him; but love itself is the transforming power.

With the love of God in our hearts we are divinely strengthened by a dynamic power and sustaining force that can truly overcome our limits and carry us into a greater existence.

It is sometimes helpful to remember the reciprocal of a truth. We will never truly possess anything we desire or strive to attain as long as we hoard it from anyone else. The height of our attainment

211

and growth is determined by how much we are willing to help others to have a chance to reach a higher level.

The great ideal was given by Jesus: " 'Truly, I say to you, as you did it to one of the least of these my brethren, you did it to me.' " (Matt. 25:40)

The good life is composed of the mutual benefits of giving and receiving. The Good Samaritan had the spirit of true living—he gave. He gave of his time, courage, physical strength, money, good will, friendship; and his giving was based on the *spirit* of the law (which breaks the bonds of the *letter* of the law).

He involved himself in a strange brotherhood. He embraced people he ordinarily would never have known or tried to know, and he became concerned and involved with them in ways that we usually reserve only for a few close friends. But it was infinitely worth all the trouble because the bonds that were broken released him into a much greater existence.

In each of us—as in the Good Samaritan—is a waiting reservoir of unfulfilled potential and unlived experience, which hounds our hearts with longings and dreams of larger life. Deep down in each of us is a spiritual "prompter"—a persistent divine urge that continually beckons and nudges us to come higher and be more, to learn and grow and express our own unique spiritual potential in all sorts of wonderful, glorious, and strange ways.

Do you want your life to flourish? Would you like a friend and companion like Jesus Christ? Remember the Good Samaritan—and *"the least of these,"* and *"go and do likewise."*

The Original Peter Principle

Dr. Laurence J. Peter, educator and author, wrote the very popular book called "The Peter Principle." He was bothered, as I think we all are, by the paradox that in spite of, or perhaps in conjunction with, all our marvelous technological advances in transportation, laborsaving devices, computers, atomic energy, and all the machinery of the goods and services of a better life, there is an almost ridiculous breakdown in the human element by which it is administrated. For example, we can now fly coast to coast in a couple of hours, but when we get there, nobody can find our luggage. Or, our appliances can automatically do nearly anything, turn themselves on or off, tune themselves, almost think for themselves; but hardly anyone can make the simplest repair on them.

Good craftsmanship and workman's pride are becoming rare. And, although computers have provided spacecraft with every possible safeguard, the difficulty of correcting one computer credit card mistake can be staggering. Several years ago, the "Unity Village News" carried a story about a Unity worker's misadventure with a credit card collection. She received a bill for $0.00 cents. She wrote several letters to point out the error, but each time she received a more demanding and abusive letter to "pay up." Inspired, she finally got an idea. She sent in a check made out for $0.00— and she never heard from them again.

Dr. Peter recognized that the incompetence and colossal blunders that constrict us exist in the human hierarchy of establishments, institutions, and organizations, which invade the privacy of almost every area of our lives—our schools, our work, our social orders, our government—all with their arrangements of ranks, grades, classes, and pyramids of leadership. As he put it: *Along with all the glorious achievements, man has produced some horrendous incompetence. He has developed bureaucracy to the point where achievement of the simplest task requires great amounts of time and effort.*

As Dr. Peter studied the hierarchies, he discovered that men and women in established organizations usually climb the ladder of success until they arrive at their respective levels of incompetence; and from this, he formulated his so-called "Peter Principle," which states: *In a hierarchy every employee tends to rise to his level of incompetence.*

Dr. Peter has written a sequel called the "Peter Prescription," which I named for myself, "A Positive Program for Protection from the Perils of the Peter Principle." I also think of his original book as, "Peter's Partial Principle." In it, he shows us why things go wrong; but, in the strictest sense, "principle" means "foundation" or "ultimate basis of cause," which implies fulfillment of right outcomes. But Dr. Peter has really hit on something. Millions have read his books, and many executives and educators have taken them quite seriously, seeking a more competent way to make things go right.

The important thing to remember in dealing with the principle is this: Incompetence is not essentially inherent in life. The universe itself is magnificently organized. As we expand our vision of space (both inner and outer), we find that all creation is uniformly organized, proceeding from one basic radiant energy into a variety of vibrational patterns, producing the atoms and molecules that are building blocks of the material universe. And for all living things organization is further evolved and brought into fulfillment according to an indwelling plan dormant in a tiny seed.

Man, the image and likeness of the Creator—in Spirit—is heir to and potentially capable of incorporating all the qualities of the cosmos into his life. But doing so isn't automatic. To develop his dormant possibilities he must learn to base his life on eternal Truth and work with the spiritual principles and laws that move all things toward fulfillment within the great universal creative plan of good.

The true spiritual foundation on which to build a better life and make things go right—spiritually—is found in what might be called the "Original Peter Principle," which follows:

Now when Jesus came into the district of Caesarea Philippi, he asked his disciples, "Who do men say that the Son of man is?" And they said, "Some say John the Baptist, others say Elijah, and others Jeremiah or one of the prophets." He said to them, "But who do you say that I am?" Simon Peter replied, "You are the Christ, the Son of the living God." And Jesus answered him, "Blessed are you, Simon Bar-Jonah! For flesh and blood has not revealed this to you, but my Father who is in heaven. And I tell you, you are Peter, and on this rock I will build my church, and the powers of death shall not prevail against it. I will give you the keys of the kingdom of heaven, and whatever you bind on earth shall be bound in heaven, and whatever you loose on earth shall be loosed in heaven." Then he strictly charged the disciples to tell no one that he was the Christ. (Matt. 16:13-20)

This is a much debated passage in the Bible. The main problem has been the word *rock* and its connection with Peter. This didn't become important at all until about A.D. 300. The early church was linked very closely to the Roman Empire, first as the object of its persecution, then conversely as

218

its official state religion. For purely administrative purposes the Roman Empire had been divided into the Eastern Roman Byzantine Empire, based in Constantinople, and the Western Roman Empire, based in Rome; and as a result, the church hierarchy also was divided. In A.D. 300 Constantinople made a great shift of the political power from Rome to Constantinople, and this greatly increased the importance of the church patriarch of Constantinople, which led the Eastern Church to challenge the supremacy of the Pope in the Western Church, producing the first major split in the church. The Western Church in Rome founded its claim for authority as the one true church on the "primacy of Peter," asserting that the passage in Matthew referred to Peter as the *rock,* designating that Jesus had appointed Peter as the head of the church. Peter had eventually traveled to Rome, and the Roman Church therefore claimed that this made it the successor to what was assumed to be the institutional power and authority given initially to Peter as the designated foundation.

James, the brother of Jesus, was said to be the presiding elder of the "First Church Council." But Peter emerged as a spokesman and leader in the early Apostolic Church.

In Bible study, we come to see how Scripture can be understood from more than one level, including both human and spiritual understanding. Going back historically, it can be appreciated why the Western Church would justify its authority and succession on the understanding that it was inherited from Peter as a former leader. It is just as easy to see why the Protestants can regard Peter as a presiding chairman, not the first divinely appointed Pope, and consider that it was the faith of Peter that was the *rock*. The apostle Paul got to the heart of the matter when he said: *For no other foundation can any one lay than that which is laid, which is Jesus Christ.* (I Cor. 3:11)

Jesus is the cornerstone of the Christian church. And the foundation of the Christ-life is the Christ Spirit. Christ is the true Rock, not Peter, not even faith. The bedrock of all spiritual work is the recognition of the divine Christ presence, the living God, which Peter suddenly intuitively discerned in Jesus. And when Jesus replied to Peter's enlightened perception—" . . . *You are the Christ, the Son of the living God"*—He was saying: "Peter, you have at last glimpsed the great fundamental Truth—I am the Christ. And it is upon this spiritual realization that my work must be built. Peter, you now have the key to all that heaven contains, the initial spiritual perception that will unlock the potential of spiritual consciousness that nothing can obstruct or defeat."

Have you ever wondered how it began with

Jesus; when and where did He first realize this tremendous truth about Himself? We might tend to believe that Jesus just always knew. But we must remember that He came into the world an infant and had to learn and grow as we do. He had to learn to walk and talk and discover and wax strong the use of His Godlike attributes. We know that at the age of twelve He had developed such a precocious grasp of Judaism that it intrigued and amazed the religious scholars in Jerusalem. The next view we have is when John the Baptist recognized Jesus as the Messiah. We don't know when Jesus recognized His own Christhood. Perhaps it came, as with Peter, in a flash. Perhaps, having learned the prophesies and promises and all the expectations of the long-awaited Messiah, one unknown, glorious day, suddenly came the blazing inspiration, "Why, I am the Messiah!"

It was the revelation of the ages. But finding ways and means to share it and to lead other people into the same realization was also one of the most difficult missions in history. It must have been very heartwarming to Jesus when, after nearly three years of teaching and demonstrating His message, one of His own disciples finally glimpsed the presence of God in Jesus and exclaimed: " . . . *You are the Christ, the Son of the living God.*" It is doubtful that Peter fully understood the divine principle that he saw in the person of Jesus, but he loved Him and believed in Him personally. And this understanding alone has worked spiritual wonders and built the faith and strengthened the lives of millions of people, just as it did in Peter.

It was the apostle Paul, however, who grew into the fuller understanding of what Jesus truly represented as the Christ. When Jesus, as a youth, received the initial revelation, "I am the Messiah," it didn't only mean to Him, "I, Jesus, am the Messiah," but I AM—the sacred ancient name of the Spirit of God in all men, the Christ—is the Messiah. The great I AM principle had been glimpsed centuries before by Moses. The supreme knowledge had come to Jesus that the same Christ Spirit that He had discovered in Himself is implanted in every child of God, and this indwelling Christ Spirit in each person is the ultimate Messiah. As Paul eventually realized and wrote in Colossians: . . . *Christ in you, the hope of glory.* (Col. 1:27)

We can far better comprehend the "Original Peter Principle" if we understand the meaning of another great Bible truth, again revealed through Paul: *Do you not know that you are God's temple and that God's Spirit dwells in you?* (I Cor. 3:16) The true Church of Christ is a state of consciousness—the Christ-life is built under the direction of the Christ within, and the first foundation step in

222

Christ consciousness is the recognition of the indwelling Christ in every human being.

In the *original* Peter principle, the object of Jesus' inquiry was to introduce His disciples to the Christ Spirit, first in Himself, then in all others, making this recognition of the indwelling divinity the basis of building and living the Christ-life. The primary objective of this principle is to lead each of us to see what Peter glimpsed in Jesus, to see it in Jesus, in ourselves, and in everyone. To the extent that the church organizations have done this, they have remained well-founded.

It should be obvious, however, that the human element of Peter's principle has also had its effect in the organization of the church. There has been a constant history of splits and divisions among the churches, all based on some difference that set them further apart, each organizing a new hierarchy of people and a new authoritarian religion, which claimed "this alone is right."

The spiritual element by which we can transcend the pitfalls of the human element in anything can be found in the principle of not only seeing what Peter saw in Jesus, but in seeing what Jesus saw in Peter—and would see in you: *You are the rock.* Each of us is symbolized in Peter— each of us can be a disciple. Each of us can become an apostle, by divine right of spiritual succession.

The church itself is built *of* individuals, as are all creative efforts. The greatness of anything comes from those qualities that constitute the greatness of an individual; and as someone once said: *"One man is just as good as another—and a great deal better."*

God didn't ask Moses to bring a committee up with him on Sinai. Committees, conferences, conventions, and counsels have brought forth many of the ideals and institutions throughout history; yet, at best, they were midwifery. Inspiration and creative ideas, the building blocks of the Christ-life, never come from groups; they are conceived and born within individuals. The Mona Lisa couldn't have been painted by a committee. The Sermon on the Mount couldn't have come from a conference report.

Every man, woman, and child is an individual, creative temple of God. The true Church is within—within the soul of each child of God. It is built— *. . . and grows into a holy temple in the Lord . . .* (Eph. 2:21)—on the creative possibilities of our latent divinity, the *kingdom* within; and it is established on the foundation of a new consciousness from which spiritual transformation becomes possible. The great fundamental truth that Jesus revealed is that God has placed His Nature in us. The world and most church organizations lack this spiritual understanding. Religious faith can be a wonderful and thrilling thing, but the sure faith can only be known through a personal spiritual awareness of the abiding power and presence of God. As H. Emilie Cady said: *There comes a time when every man must stand alone with his God.*

God is never really found in a place, nor even a ritual or a ceremony. God is found in a state of consciousness. To worship Him in spirit and truth is to recognize the truth of His spiritual presence in us and base our lives on the spiritual square one of the universe: *"I AM that I AM,"* the great principle of Christhood—God's Nature implanted in every person.

The revelation . . . *Christ in you, the hope of glory* takes nothing away from Jesus. Only a Christ could fully reveal the Christ Spirit. It only accents the magnificence of His Sonship. In addition, it greatly expands our relationship with the Father within and multiplies His influence and triumphant power through us. The "Original Peter Principle" elaborates the great Truth hidden through the ages: God indwells us. The same Christ Spirit that was in Jesus is implanted in you. The great principle of life—the key to the kingdom of heaven is: Find that Christ in yourself. And upon this rock of recognition He will build His church, the Christ-life in you.

Acting Out Abundance

This is a magnificent universe, an opulent, abundant universe. But it is also unfinished. God has completed the all-important spiritual side (the kingdom of His potential). He has also set in motion a universal creation process, supported by an ever-available supply of infinite latent qualities. And, He has seen to it that it is guided by a master plan of good toward the perfect manifestation of a glorious divine purpose.

God has also intrinsically involved each of us in His creative process. As his spiritual image and likeness, the fullness of His potential and the capstone of His nature are vested in us. (As Jesus plainly said, " . . . *the kingdom of God is in the midst of you.*" [within] A.V. (Luke 17:20)

This chapter is about God's waiting repository of spiritual resources in us. It is based on Jesus' story, found in the book of Matthew, called "The Parable of the Talents." The parable is about the kingdom of heaven. (*Heaven* comes from a root word that conveys expanding potential.) This story compares the kingdom of heaven to a rich man with three servants. The master of the house, before going away on a long journey, gave each of his three servants money to invest and increase for him while he was away. To one servant he gave five talents, to another three, and to the third one.

This parable is sometimes confused with another one recorded in Luke which is much like it except that it is in terms of *pounds*. The only significant difference in this story is that the master gave the servants *equal* amounts of money to invest. In both parables, when the master returned, he demanded an accounting of the investment that the servants were to have gained by trading. In the "Parable of the Talents," two servants doubled their investments. In the "Parable of the Pounds," two servants also did very well in increasing their amounts: one by ten pounds, another by five. To all these successful servants in both stories, the master essentially said: "Well done, good and faithful servants. You have been faithful over a few things, I will now make you ruler of many things. Enter into the joy of the Lord." But also in both stories is the example of a servant who did nothing because he was afraid to lose what he already had. In both cases, the master rebuked the unsuccessful servant and took away what originally had been given him, giving it instead to the servants who had succeeded.

Both stories end: *"For to every one who has will more be given, and he will have abundance; but from him who has not, even what he has will be taken away."* (Matt. 25:29) Matthew continues:

"And [he] cast the worthless servant into the outer darkness; there men will weep and gnash their teeth." (Matt. 25:30)

We can conclude several things from these two parables. First, God endows in each of us spiritual investments—latent potentials and qualities of His nature that constitute our essential talents. Perhaps in the Parable of the Pounds we are meant to realize that in the beginning we are all created equal. That, as the United States Constitution says, we are all given equal spiritual endowments, as God's image. We are created equal, but we were not born equal nor do we stay equal. The Parable of the Talents deals with this extended aspect. Remember that in these two parables, Jesus is teaching us something important about the kingdom of spiritual potential originally vested in us and its development in us.

He is telling us that, from a spiritual perspective, God has given each of us extraordinary gifts and extraordinary qualities of Spirit that can be used by us in developing our lives. If we make right use of them, we shall become more like Him, and we shall find life increasing in meaning, beauty, and value.

Among the richest gifts are those represented by the twelve powers. All these twelve gifts of Spirit are on loan to us from God, and we are to use the creativity of Jesus Christ to develop them.

As He said, " . . . *the Father who dwells in me does his works.*" (John 14:10) But He also said: *"My Father is working still, and I am working."* (John 5:17)—a Father-Son creative partnership! God's contribution is infinitely greater than ours, but our part is very important too.

The emphasis of these two parables of Jesus is not on the amount of the gifts, but on how we use what we have. The principle of the kingdom of heaven is growth, the evolution of spiritual potential. The law of life, therefore, is use or lose. This is true on every level of life, be it physical, mental, emotional, social, or financial. And of course it is true on the spiritual level.

It is the very nature of our endowments, attributes, and talents (no matter how great or small) to be used and shared or they become worthless. When we bury any asset with nonuse, we lose all benefits from it.

Unused talents are like a sundial in the shade. We are never rewarded in life according to our talents, but rather according to what we do with them. Abilities and capacities always grow with wise use, and it is true that those who have get more, and those who have not lose what they have. If we have gained knowledge, it is inevitable that we will receive more. The same is true with physical strength, friends, opportunities, peace, tolerance, forgiveness, love—any and all the qualities and attributes of life.

They are all developed and multiplied by use and lost by nonuse. Each of us has many talents; yet, if we have only one talent of which we are aware, and we use it, it will open to us "the windows of heaven." It will open us up to the fullness of life and all its possibilities.

Perhaps you wonder what your latent talents are. Each of them is a way to express God, to express good in your life. They first take form within as, for example, constructive, benevolent, truth-filled thoughts and feelings. They find expression as cheerful, optimistic, friendly, creative, loving words and actions.

We are not to worry or make an issue about what we do not have; we are to do our best with what we do have—we are to use well the Truth we know today.

The following once appeared in Unity's DAILY WORD:

Some years ago an ancient building was razed from its site in England. The new building project for which the location was cleared was delayed. In the meantime, the sunshine and rain upon the bare ground caused plants to grow and flower that were not indigenous to England soil. Naturalists came to examine the plants and identified some as coming from seed of plants which the Romans had brought to that land two thousand years before.

All of us have latent talents that have not been nurtured or exposed to light and stimulation. Discovering these talents is an invigorating experience in the adventure of living.

We can increase our confidence in the skills we already have by putting more love into our present work and cultivating an attitude of gratitude. Right now we can make the most of possibilities and opportunities that present themselves. And we can have confidence that we are being led into the right environment where our abilities and faculties are needed and appreciated.

Talents are the seeds of God's creative possibilities in each of us. We all have them, but they must be germinated and cultivated. Most people give up far too soon. We have become a nation of spectators who live vicariously through the "great" and the "famous." This is a mistaken emphasis. In our hearts, we would all like to be extraordinary people; but, in Jesus' approach to life, the promise is that ordinary people can do extraordinary things!

Jesus once pointed out that the ordinary became extraordinary by going the extra mile. Most of us are willing to do our fair share, but nothing ever changes that way. Progress is made by those who add something extra to the ordinary and, therefore, they become extraordinary.

The scribes and pharisees had but one job, to keep things the way they were—to go to any lengths to maintain the status quo. But we can never successfully do that, for then we bury our own possibilities and all the promises of the future.

To gain the kingdom of heaven, and to practice the creativity of Jesus, we have to be willing to try something exceptional and not just "get by." A real Truth student is an exceptional person who should always be doing exceptional things.

It is of course all a matter of consciousness. We must continually learn to stretch our consciousness, to go the extra mile, to accomplish exceptional and extraordinary transformations in our own beliefs and attitudes, and to express unique and creative manifestations in our lives.

Jesus linked the lessons of the talents and pounds to something material—money and finances. He knew that they represent a powerful control in our deep underlying convictions—that where our treasure is, so are our hearts. We can easily get entrapped in the wrong attitudes about money. Yet, Jesus knew that, because of what it does command in us, we can also use our concepts about money to uplift our lives.

Our attitudes about finances have a great effect on our health, security, self-image, and on our total life experience. Jesus talked about abundant life. Abundance, from His point of view, has far less to do with the money we have than it does with our attitudes about it. True riches are the riches of consciousness. Jesus' point in using monetary units in His illustrations about spiritual resources is that if we change our attitudes about material possessions for the better, we can change our lives considerably.

How many talents are hidden in you? You can get a glimmer if you will accept Jesus' promise: *"Truly, truly, I say to you, he who believes in me will also do the works that I do; and greater works than these will he do, because I go to the Father."* (John 14:12) Paul reveals the staggering implications of our own divinity in his insight: . . . *this mystery, which is Christ in you, the hope of glory.* (Col. 1:27)

How do we discover these unsuspected talents? Shakespeare advised: *Assume a virtue, if you have it not.* Ovid elaborated: *The virtue which lies hidden unrecognized in times of prosperity, asserts itself in adversity.* Don't wait until your "ship comes in," learn to act out abundance—the opulent, abundant treasure of talents of Christ in you.

All life proceeds from within. To rise above your present level of consciousness about life, stretch your thinking above its average level—use the dynamic law of spiritual increase. Begin to think, feel, and act as though you now had the abundance in your life that you wish you had. Begin in your consciousness to stir up gifts of God within you by being loyal to your divine inheritance. Start remembering who you are—a child of God. Learn to think in terms of the qualities within you rather than situations, events, and circumstances without—the qualities that can be seen in Jesus Christ, who, by being totally oriented to the kingdom of heaven and the Father within, was the co-creator with the Father of the best life that has ever been lived. Practice identifying the divine qualities of life, intelligence, power, love, and goodness as yours to use—ready and waiting right within you. Use well what you now have, and the Father will increasingly reward you with greater expression. Tell yourself, "I am a child of God, I am rich with the riches of the kingdom of heaven and all its divine potential." Think, talk, and act in the name of Jesus—the consciousness of Jesus Christ.

This is not pretending or trying to be something you are not. It is affirming and expressing a little more of what you really are in Spirit and Truth. It works for everyone and anyone who will apply it.

One of the most delightful and adventurous dramas we can experience in our personal lives is the discovery of a hidden talent. But it is also one of life's grandest fruitions to use a familiar talent in a good and faithful way.

Especially use your often neglected talent of

positive, constructive, and creative thinking. Use also your Godlike talent of creative imagination to act out the "life more abundant" that Jesus Christ talked about. Stretch your consciousness a little every day. Go the extra mile; dare to try something new, different, exceptional, and extraordinary. You will find that the market places of life will open themselves to what you have to offer. Above all, learn to give of yourself, and you will receive much more than you can ever give, because you can't outgive God!

Oh, That Paul!

The accusation nailed to Jesus' Cross was written in three languages: Greek, Latin, and Hebrew. These three world powers dramatically converged at the inception of Christianity. Of all the pioneer Christians, the great apostle Paul most vividly belonged to all three of these streams of culture and history.

He had been born and raised a Jew, Saul of Tarsus. This Mediterranean harbor city, which contributed substantially to the broadening of young Saul's education, was a perfect example of cosmopolitan Hellenism, itself a blend of the classical Greek and oriental mysticism. In addition, Paul had been born a first-class Roman citizen. This privileged status was inherited from his father, who had apparently done an outstanding public service for the Roman Empire, possibly for Anthony and Cleopatra on their infamous rendezvous at Tarsus.

All three of these factors had a formidable influence in molding Paul's consciousness as the original missionary "statesman," apostle to the Gentiles, and founding father of Christology and all its ensuing doctrines and dogmas.

Gaining a perspective as to how and why these divergent influences came into Paul's life can be very important to us, for these now deeply imbedded persuasions (social, moral, and political, as well as religious) were all brought together and introduced into Christianity by Paul. Jesus had been the spiritual author, but Paul became the great propagator and chief architect of Christianity's religious systems. Indeed, we know more about Paul than we do Jesus, because a considerable part of the New Testament consists of Paul's letters and activities. Paul, the Apostle, was not only the most dynamic and influential of early Christians, but much of present-day Christianity can definitely be said to be "Pauline."

It was of course the Hebrew tradition that was most formidable in the development of young Saul. His parents instilled and kept alive in him a deep love for Judaism, the religion of the Jewish people. As a youth, he had been trained in the strict observance of the Pharisees, a society of zealous scholars who believed that everything was fulfilled by keeping the Torah, the body of Jewish religious law. The Judaism of Saul gave him a strong devotion to *the law of the fathers*. The word "law" occurs 118 times in his Epistles. As were all young Jews, Paul was also given training in a practical trade—his was tent cloth-making— which later served him very well in supporting himself in his missionary work. His devotion to the religion of his forefathers was so great that at the age of about twenty he was admitted to the rabbinical school of the Pharisees in Jerusalem to study under the famous Gamaliel.

Perhaps his strict Jewish upbringing prevented Saul from receiving a complete formal Greek education (Tarsus was a university city—home of leading stoic philosophies), but he spoke Greek as well as Hebrew and became very learned in the life and intellectuality of a Greek-Hellenistic city. This can be seen in the contrast between the rural and provincial illustrations of Jesus (sheep, seeds, rising bread) and the city life metaphors that Paul uses (statues, theatre, the stadium, courts of justice, and the marketplace).

Paul's language sometimes reflects Greek philosophy and the stoic teaching in words like "nature," "conscience," and "sufficiency," and he also used the esoteric vocabulary of the mystery-religions (including "the deep things of God," *the mystery of Christ, the hidden wisdom, "that which no eye has seen nor ear heard," a mirror dimly, the mind of Christ, the inner man, the temple of the Holy Spirit within you, the resurrection of the dead*, and, as we shall see, his ultimate realization about *the mystery hidden for ages*, which, to Charles Fillmore, were the greatest words ever written).

Of great significance, Paul became a proponent of the teachings of Aristotle, and firmly instituted

Christianity in the philosophical framework of his third-dimensional materialistic interpretation of the universe, the basis of such characteristically strongly guarded religious dogma as the finite person/places doctrinal concepts of the "Trinity," "heaven," and "hell." Only very recently has Einstein's revolutionary new insight of the universe broken through Aristotelian limits and united a dynamic new physics with the ancient wisdom of metaphysics.

It was the Roman influence that gave Paul his pragmatic drive. As a Roman citizen he learned to appreciate what Rome contributed to the world in its time: the material benefits of its far-flung roads, aqueducts, and harbors, and the stability and control of its worldwide commonwealth of law and order. (Paul once appealed to distant Rome for justice even in Jerusalem.) Paul's Roman citizenship often got him out of trouble in his missionary travels, and he considered it one of his prized possessions.

More important, however, it was Paul's affinity with Rome that brought about a fervent zeal for winning the Roman Empire for Jesus Christ and compelled him to concentrate his missionary campaign in often dangerous centers of strong Roman influence.

So, Paul's consciousness was a blend—Jewish, Greek, and Roman—and throughout his writing

we find a curious mixture of Old Testament thinking, mysticism, philosophy, and practical, empiri-
cal logic. To that we must add the formidable
influence of the personality through which these
shifting perceptions were expressed. Paul was a
fascinating person. He had a brilliant mind, alert
with keen reasoning power, and alive with vivid
imagination. He also possessed a great heart, full
of devotion and, often, tenderness. He also had
burning ambition, and overactive will, and ways
that were sometimes irritating and often exasper-
ating. Paul was obviously chosen by God for a
great mission, but Paul tended to get ahead of the
plan, and not even the Holy Spirit could always
hold this dauntless missionary to the divine intent.

Paul was an organizer, a builder of institutions,
and a rule-maker. He translated the simple spiritual teachings of Jesus into a complex, worldly,
ecclesiastical institution. He far surpassed the
original disciples in spreading Christianity to the
"ends of the earth," but he often used his personal
magnetism and strong persuasive powers to expe-
dite local and particular problems into narrow and
parochial solutions. It left a dichotomy. Much of
the oppressive emphasis on sin and the distressing
dark side of religion was introduced into the radiant teachings of Jesus by Paul. Jesus revealed to
mankind a positive, liberating way of life. He
pointed us inward and gave us encouraging prom-

ises and examples of what we can become. Paul often fell short of this with admonitions about what not to do and the insistence on restrictive outward observances. (Perhaps you have noticed how those in denominational hassles and religionists preoccupied with enforcing the negatives of theology almost always support their positions with quotes from Paul rather than Jesus.)

Primarily, we need to reinterpret Paul according to Jesus. And in doing so, we need to establish our perspective within the context of the most overlooked—and yet ultimately the most significant—influence in Paul's life: the growing influence of the living Christ within Paul. A main consideration to observe in the remarkable drama of Paul's life is his own growth: the development of spiritual consciousness and spiritual discernment, his discovery of life's great secret of spiritual Oneness, and God as a loving universal Father, and his final realization of the indwelling Christ—in everyone.

Some of the spiritual conversion in Paul's life happened in a flash, but much was an evolving, maturing transformation throughout the rest of his life.

Throughout his life, Paul was very human. Wonderfully so, just like us! He lived a real life, and his experiences were quite genuine. He made mistakes (once referring to himself as the *foremost*

244

of sinners). Paul was a complex man and he experienced deep human emotions. He was often in opposition to people—and quick to criticize—yet his letters were sometimes masterpieces of love. As we shall see, Paul had soul-searching low points and frequently suffered hardship, persecution, turmoil, and anxiety. And as he grew, he was sometimes in conflict with his own former self. Yet he was unsinkable and emerged ultimately the dominating figure in every situation, a giant of strength and courage.

Paul first appeared in the Bible as Saul the persecutor. The drama had all begun with Jesus, whom Paul never saw. His amazing part of the Christian story started with his involvement in the death of a member of the small troublesome cult of Jesus' post-Crucifixion followers, Stephen. When Saul saw Stephen die, and heard the haunting words, " . . . *Lord, do not hold this sin against them,"* (Acts 7:59) something began to work in his heart.

We next see him at the head of a column of Temple soldiers pursuing those followers of Jesus who had fled to Damascus. It was on the road to Damascus that he was literally knocked off his horse by a blinding, life-changing vision. Saul had started that trip a proud young man, with all the pomp and circumstance of a conquering hero leading a small army. He ended the trip by being led into Damascus by the hand like a blind beggar.

Everything Saul had ever possessed up to that time was suddenly wiped away. All the bridges to his past were burned. To his fellow Jews, he was a turncoat. His relationship with his family was completely severed. And even by the followers of Jesus, he was suspected as a spy.

Yet, this drastic reversal became the great event in his life, because as a result he became an apostle to Jesus Christ. And soon, in Damascus, another very significant thing happened that also worked in the heart of Paul for the rest of his life. A man named Ananias, at first very reluctantly, was inspired to help Saul. And Saul, blind, helpless, and utterly desolate, felt a hand on his shoulder and heard the words: *"Brother Saul . . . ."* (Acts 9:17) And Saul knew the love of Christ!

With the help of his friends in Christ, Saul soon escaped from Damascus, over the city wall in a garbage basket. He retreated to the wilderness (Petra), and there is then a three-year gap in his life. Undoubtedly, it included introspection, prayer, and meditation, which allowed the original conversion experience to gather strength and stability.

Then he again appeared in Jerusalem, set to go. But he was a maverick, and he soon learned that the disciples in Jerusalem had no place in their plans for him.

He went back home to Tarsus, not to his parents, but into complete seclusion, undoubtedly to lick his wounds. After a time, Barnabas, one of the few Jerusalem followers of Jesus who had been impressed by Saul, sought him out of his seclusion and invited him to join in a missionary journey.

This was the first of three (perhaps four) great missionary journeys that led Paul (his name was changed early in the first journey) thousands of miles into unknown lands in which he established Christian converts all the way to Rome and brought Christianity to Europe (they were first called "Christians" in Antioch—at that time, a derisive term for this strange cult of "little Christs"). It is important to note that in A.D. 637 the Moslems invaded Jerusalem, and if it had not been for Paul's tenacious effort to take the message west, we might never have heard of Christianity.

Here are some other important things to remember about Paul's missionary work. His epistles were not written by him as Holy Scripture, but as letters to friends. They are chronicles of his personal experiences, of the advice he gave others in various situations, and of his own growth and unfoldment. Much of the drama of these memorable writings is from the undercurrent of the feud he had with the Jerusalem disciples, who had so quickly developed the notion of orthodoxy and church authority; and, instead of following Jesus' instructions to take the message into all the world, had settled into a holding operation awaiting Jesus' return and the end of the world. As they waited, they digressed into the temporal and banal concerns typical of most religious arguments and quarrels. A major issue centered around whether Gentiles had to become Jews before they could be Christians. Paul wanted to convert everybody. The disciples in Jerusalem did not consider Paul "legitimate," because he had never known Jesus personally (which may have been his "thorn in the flesh"). Therefore, they discredited and undercut him at every step. His theology was no good, he was a troublemaker and—their accusation to the Romans—a peacebreaker.

Paul countered with the position that he was an apostle of the "risen Christ," and that his authority was the Christ Spirit. It took Paul quite a little growth to realize himself exactly what this meant, but as the one person who most interpreted Jesus for us, it is vitally important for us to understand that Paul eventually gained the spiritual awareness that could perceive Jesus' message as entirely spiritual and realize that the spiritual experience he himself had on the road to Damascus was a classic example of how Christ returns—spiritually—as a living presence within ourselves.

In this, Paul eventually awakened to the spiritual reality (Jesus' kingdom of Spirit) behind and beyond Aristotle's outer-based perception of the world, and gradually came to appreciate that the "fruits of Spirit" are gained from within and not from without ourselves.

As with the Jerusalem disciples, much of Paul's missionary campaign was also based on an interim ethic of outer behavior. But he outgrew the judgmental morality for which he is often remembered—and quoted—and became foremost a mystic, a spiritual-minded man of prayer, the first follower of Christ to say that the truly authentic experience of religion (to "worship in Spirit and Truth") is a direct, intimate communion with God's abiding Spirit, a mystical union with the Christ of God in us. Paul's original dependence on law as an exoteric control was gradually transmuted into a metaphysical trust in the creative activity that can come forth from the Spirit of God in man.

Paul summed up his spiritual insight and gave his highest vision in his Epistle to the Colossians *(the mystery hidden for ages . . .) Christ in you, the hope of glory.* (Col. 1:26, 27) With it was the exalted realization that Jesus came as the great Way-Shower so that we may be like Him—by following Him on the inward path of spiritual unfoldment—to be . . . *changed into his likeness from one degree of glory to another; for this comes from the Lord who is the Spirit.* (II Cor. 3:18)

This chapter has been about Paul. The next three, based on his life, will be about us. He has left his mark on each of us. Almost every human in the Western world has been influenced by Paul's understanding of Jesus Christ. Few other men have set up such conflicts of love and dissension. But it was love and not the rigid, narrow doctrines and gloomy theology of Paul that became the great force in his own life. Probably because of Ananias in Damascus, he wrote in a letter to the Romans: . . . *in everything God works for good with those who love him* . . . . (Rom. 8:28) He showed us, in spite of all prevailing human and personal shortcomings, what Spirit can do to a person. He is a believable, exciting, touching example of a spiritual transformation in a human being. The really exciting thing about Paul's dramatic life is that it can happen to us.

There is an element of mystery surrounding the latter days of Paul's life. He may have been acquitted in his trial at Rome and had a fourth journey that took him as far as Britain, later to be executed in Nero's persecution.

But he had learned that, in Christ, death is swallowed up in victory. By perceiving . . . *the*

mystery which was kept secret for long ages . . . .
(Rom. 16:25) he had come to know Christ intimately, as an eternal, indwelling presence—our
own eternal Self.

Of greatest value to us, probably, is that Paul
often practiced what he preached. Once, he admonished the Philippians: *Have this mind among
yourselves, which is yours in Christ Jesus . . . .*
(Phil. 2:5) Paul had literally achieved a high
degree of Christ consciousness. He had truly lived
out his counsel to the Colossians to: *. . . put on
the new nature, which is being renewed in knowledge after the image of its creator.* (Col. 3:10)

What a man! What a life! In his acquired mystical attitude about life, Paul wrote to those in
Rome:

*For I am sure that neither death, nor life, nor
angels, nor principalities, nor things present, nor
things to come, nor powers, nor height, nor
depth, nor anything else in all creation, will be
able to separate us from the love of God in Christ
Jesus our Lord.* (Rom. 8:38)

And friends, when you understand what Paul
meant by *that*, you will know, as he did, what life
is all about.

The Grand Encounter

We have been introduced to one of the most extraordinary, unforgettable Christians of all times, the apostle Paul. As a religious pioneer of Christianity, Paul did much to take Jesus' spiritual message into all corners of the world, and also to alter it into a complicated, ecclesiastical organization. But the greatest importance of Paul to us can be his example as a spiritual pioneer. A study of the great lessons and adventures in his personal life can help us learn to meet the challenges and opportunities we encounter on our pathway to spiritual growth.

We will now explore the most memorable encounter in Paul's remarkable life, his "Damascus Road Experience," the spiritual conversion that changed him from Saul to Paul.

There was nothing lukewarm about Paul. Whatever he did, he did "breathing flame," and moved ahead full throttle. When he took up the cause against the sect of fledgling Christians, he not only became a persecutor but sought to become *chief* persecutor.

Persecuting the Christians seems like such a terrible thing to us, but the motives and determination of Saul were utterly sincere. The followers of the man Jesus were seen by Saul as enemies of the worst kind (much the same as Christians would later feel about numerous factions and groups that seemed to rival their particular denomination). To Saul these were heretical enemies of all that the Pharisees stood for—all the truth that he studied, honored, and loved as a Jew—enemies boring within the ancient Mosaic fabric, threatening to destroy it.

And then—something happened! In one incredible moment, Saul's life and history—right down to us—was changed forever.

Here is the account as recorded in Acts 9:3-9: *Now as he journeyed he approached Damascus, and suddenly a light from heaven flashed about him. And he fell to the ground and heard a voice saying to him, "Saul, Saul, why do you persecute me?" And he said, "Who are you, Lord?" And he said, "I am Jesus, whom you are persecuting; but rise and enter the city, and you will be told what to do." The men who were traveling with him stood speechless, hearing the voice but seeing no one. Saul arose from the ground; and when his eyes were opened, he could see nothing; so they led him by the hand and brought him into Damascus. And for three days he was without sight, and neither ate nor drank.*

What had happened? It was "The Grand Encounter," a rare, hard to explain, seemingly uninvited and instantaneous spiritual experience sometimes called "conversion," a powerful, trans-forming moment of deep surrender and rebirth that changes a person and makes all the difference in everything. Saul had a blazing, "blind" encounter with the living Presence. The voice he heard was Christ, introducing him into an entirely new dimension of existence, saying, in effect, "Here is what your soul has been seeking such a long, long time, the truth that I AM. Here I AM, a new vision in which the world looks different, with new values, new goals, new experiences of Truth, beauty, joy, love, and grace—a new, exciting life for the old one."

Saul had experienced what has recently been labeled a "paradigm shift," a sudden experience in altered consciousness, entry into the spiritual, cosmic Christ consciousness that is the Saviour of the world, that mind that was in Christ Jesus, which disclosed to Saul the divine way and his own divine possibilities.

As mysterious as they seem, conversions are primarily experiences in consciousness—a new mind with new ideas and a new way of thinking. They open us up to new resources, new energies, new qualities right within ourselves. They bring forth healing, creativity, and the waiting potentials of our true nature. They can seem sudden and startling, like bolts of lightning. But lightning isn't really sudden at all; it is the culmination of mighty forces that have long been gathering.

Cardinal Newman wrote that there are really no sudden conversions, but there are sudden realizations that you now *are* what you have already become through hard work.

What is conversion? From Cardinal Newman's observation, we can see that it is a change within that has been born in our minds and proclaims itself to us in a new vision. A conversion is a new awareness, a new way of seeing, a new state of consciousness. Conversion is a discovery of something that has been happening within, a spiritual influence that has long been at work. If the discovery is instantaneous (one great moment), the event is dramatic, emotionally impactive, often impassioned. The change can also occur almost imperceptibly as a gradual, creative, inner development that progressively "makes us over."

Whether the awakening is sudden or subtle, it is really a continuing, cumulative process of inner spiritual evolution, transcending, regenerating, and uplifting us into new dimensions, new possibilities, and amazing new adventures. And it is always very personal—and universal.

Saul's classic conversion, unique and personal to him, was a prototype spiritual transformation. It was the natural result of the "leaven" of all the years of study, prayer, and the Truth seeking that had gathered in him since childhood. With him, it became a "blinding light," flooding every nook and cranny of his consciousness with a radiant illumination that initiated a life-changing, spiritual rebirth.

It was the authentic spiritual encounter from which he later observed: *Therefore, if any one is in Christ, he is a new creation; the old has passed away, behold, the new has come.* (II Cor. 5:17)

Baby turtles have a seemingly uncanny ability to find the ocean. A Harvard professor discovered that they can neither see, nor hear, nor even smell the ocean, but they are attracted by the light. They always go to the ocean because there is more light there than toward the land. There is something inside the turtle that makes him want to go where he can find the most light.

Each of us is a creation of light, and deep within each of us is a longing to unfold in the direction of more light.

Most of Saul's young life had been dedicated to the religious life according to the understanding of the established beliefs of his time. But the Lord of Saul's being knew that he had grown to a level where he was ready for new enlightenment. And, for Saul, at the perfect time, illumination came as a great surprise to him.

Spiritual experiences are natural experiences. We are, essentially, spiritual beings. When Saul's soul was ready, he received that portion of his spiritual heritage that was exactly necessary and appropriate for his next level of growth and unfoldment. And, although it seemed to be accomplished by the sensational, spectacular lightning clamor of a Wagnerian opera, its real work had been done as quietly and simply as the growth of grass—or better, the growth of a child.

There have been many spiritual experiences throughout history—classical episodes such as Abraham's "call," Moses and the burning bush, Jacob's double encounter with the ladder and the wrestling angel, Peter's sudden insight into the Christ nature of Jesus, and even Jesus' own Transfiguration. Each of these contributed to our evolving understanding of true, spiritual, latent Christ-potential in all people. There have been many lesser known Spirit-revealing experiences that have occurred in every land of every age, often not strictly religious experiences, but transcending encounters with a mysterious spiritual X factor that transformed the minds and hearts of artists, poets, musicians, government leaders, scientists, farmers, and housewives, each revealing higher and nobler expressions of the possibilities of our true nature.

We each have our own soul pattern, our own individual plan for growth and unfoldment. Therefore, we all develop differently and have different experiences. The exact manner of our life-changing transformations are unique and peculiar to each of us, but they are bound to come to any seeker of Truth. If we are alert, we will discover that we experience fresh encounters daily.

Spiritual attainment is more than an event. It is a way of life, a way of seeking more light. The vision opens our eyes. The world looks different; life becomes sacred; God's presence exhibits *every bush aflame;* what heretofore appeared separate and divided becomes unified, and differences tend to be resolved and transcended. Best of all, *we* increase in spirit and Truth. We go beyond what we have been to more of what we can be. Our illusions, fears, inhibitions, and defenses decrease and are replaced by the qualities of Christ.

What happens—in every case, whether it be called conversion, paradigm shift, peak experience, born again, grand encounter, inspiration, intuition, creativity, cosmic consciousness, illumination, whole-brain experience, healing, or a spiritual experience—is simply some degree of awakening in our consciousness to the reality of what is as God created it from our belief of what is as we have formulated it in our lesser comprehension. Each is an encounter with a new idea, a new perception of Truth, a new identity with love, life, peace, joy, power, beauty—with God.

Each encounter with higher consciousness is as

important as any other. None is permanent. Each one challenges us to a new level of living. From each one we are reborn from Spirit.

Paul's encounter—a great blazing moment—was a rare and beautiful vision of Christ. We each share in his living realization, as all humanity shares in each awakening we experience.

It is often difficult for us to believe in human nature when it is pitted against the stark challenges of our present human experiences that we now so persistently confuse with reality. But we are not required to believe in human nature—as we now understand it. All we need to believe in is God's indwelling, transforming power in every person—the Christ!

Our friend Paul was a marvelous example of what God can do with a human being.

Those Magnificent Defeats

Sometimes I reminisce and play a little game of "what if," knowing that in my life, as in all others, there have been times when things could have gone a different way. I pick a turning point where, if another choice or decision or preference had been made, or an alternate course of events or circumstances had occurred, or if the "breaks" (as we sometimes call the seeming chances of life) had just gone the "right way" at a certain time, my life might have been—if. Since my discovery of Unity, I have also learned by retrospect that often what have seemed times of painful disappointment have turned out to be divine appointments, leading to a wonderful rendezvous with some unforeseen good. Somehow these speculative returns to the past have increased my appreciation and trust of the divine element that shapes our ends.

The life of the great apostle Paul, with his amazing influence on all of us, lends itself well to the "what if" perception. What would have happened if Paul had not experienced that sudden and surprising spiritual turning point on the road to Damascus? What would have happened to Christianity? What would history have been like? Certainly the experience completely changed everything in his life!

If you recall, Paul, up to that time, had a marvelous life from the human point of view. He had all the worldly advantages of "high birth"—wealth, education, prestige, and influence. Indeed, Paul had almost everything that almost everyone of every society of every age ever wanted in life. Then he had one encounter with the living Christ. What a change it made in everything! It changed him, Christianity, history, and us.

Without that one turning point, it is reasonable to assume that Paul would have continued his persecution of the early Christians. We will never know what difference that might have made in the success of the persecution and the possible elimination of the Christians. We do know that without Paul Christianity may never have broken out of Judaism and spread to the Western world.

The most authenticated consequences of the Damascus Road turning point is the drama of change in Paul's own life. In a blinding flash, Paul was wrenched from one life and inaugurated into an entirely new existence. In this single instance, he was stripped of almost all he possessed or held dear in the world—wealth, position, protection, comfort, friends, and family. The table was turned, and it was Paul instead who was vulnerable to persecution, danger, hardship, humiliation, and martyrdom. He became a target of painful, personal abuse and degradation with insults, lies, and slander. All in all, from our own human perspective, this "reversal" in Paul's life would seem to be one of the most tragic and cruel defeats possible.

We of course know that these "defeats" produced a magnificent, triumphant life—a new life for an old one.

The reason Paul can be such an inspiration to us is not because he was a man who didn't make any mistakes or fail at anything, but because he was a man who—with God's help—brought victory out of defeat, time and time again!

Paul loved every aspect and possibility of the new life he found in Christ, and he wrote about it from many angles; but he never said it was easy. It is often difficult for Truth students too. It is not only hard to apply and hold to the Truth, but often downright painful in adjusting to the process of change that often purges our lives before it improves them. (Dr. H. Emilie Cady called it "chemicalization.")

Some of Paul's most inspiring writings were the letters of encouragement he wrote out of his own experience to his missionary converts, helping them to understand the challenges and obstacles of this new path.

He often pointed out his own shortcomings and

the times he had failed to accomplish the things he had wanted so much to do: . . . *For I do not do what I want, but I do the very thing I hate.* (Romans 7:15) This is probably why Paul is so important to us. He went through the same things we do, and we can gain strength, courage, and new resolve in knowing that he overcame these things.

How many times do we catch ourselves thinking negative thoughts when we don't want to think negative thoughts at all? How many times do we find ourselves falling back into old negative habits and reactions when we don't want to do anything negative or be negative in any way?

When these things happen, we are apt to become discouraged and not like ourselves very well. Once, when Paul felt this way, he wrote: *Wretched man that I am! Who will deliver me from this body of death?* (Romans 7:24)

Do you ever get frustrated, even wretched, about your spiritual resolves, wondering if you are ever going to become the kind of person you want to be?

The Bible has many wonderful examples of success that occurred when somebody aligned himself with God. We often tend to think we are "right" with God when we have succeeded in some endeavor. Conversely, failure at least vaguely suggests some kind of alienation with

God. Fortunately, for our own best interests, we sometimes do fail! You see, God's plan is often quite different from ours (even Jesus prayed: " . . . *nevertheless not my will, but thine, be done*"). (Luke 22:42)

It isn't that we should ever make failure a goal. It is just that we must recognize that failure is usually a part of the way in which we grow. God doesn't provide us with failures (we are quite capable of doing that for ourselves), but God can use our failures in His plan of good. And what we think of as failure can often play a vital role in the process by which we are transformed.

The human state is not the state of perfection. The human state is the overcoming, transforming state. We are in this life to learn and grow. We do so best by finding God's plan for us and following it. It is by no means easy; yet learning, growing, overcoming, and experiencing transformation can be one of life's greatest joys! (It *certainly* makes life interesting!)

Failure is painful. It hurts in the vicinity of the human ego. But the great thing about God's gift to us of our humanity is that He made marvelous provisions in His plan for ultimate success by which we can make mistakes in using our endowment of free choice—and then grow from these very mistakes.

In historical retrospect, we can see that many

things that were considered tragic and destroying became transforming and highly beneficial in human advancement. What if we couldn't make mistakes? We wouldn't be here. The human race would have been destroyed long ago.

Correcting mistakes and the wrong choices of free will plays a large part in the development of every child. Children gradually discover the world they live in and their own faculties and abilities by a series of experiences of failure. By falling, children learn to walk. Through many misunderstandings they experiment, test, and rectify these perceptions, and they learn to express themselves better. ("I want to do it myself!") Their early rapid rate of learning is surely coupled with their lack of inhibition and false pride in making mistakes—when they fall, they get right up and try again.

An adolescent, sometimes with impulsive enthusiasm, will experience many failures which teach him important lessons in maturing.

Even national crises and the shock of unexpected catastrophes and defeats can open a country's eyes—first to its mistakes and then to its new opportunities—and unite its people, giving them the surge of energy needed to rise to new heights.

Nowhere in life does anyone experience only success. Throughout the Bible, side by side with promises of guidance and success within God's upward, onward plan for fulfillment, we find promises of grace and providential corrections for our deviations within the sacred gift of free choice. Clearly, in our soul growth and spiritual unfoldment, failure plays its part in our true success.

Looking back, we see that in Abraham's call and the covenant of the Promised Land, God didn't promise him a rose garden. Canaan would have to be taken by a series of conquests and defeats, and gradually settled by his descendants over a long period of time. (Its promise has not really been fulfilled yet!)

Moses encountered a burning bush, a visionary promise of divine help. The bush itself was an ancient symbol of painful trials and difficulties (from the flesh wounds inflicted by thorns). The symbol of a bush that burned but was not consumed was the promise that Moses' mission would ultimately triumph, though there might be many times of difficulty, suffering, and temporary defeat. Much of the drama in the Bible is elaboration on this theme—the magnificence that God can call forth from our "defeats."

The greatest drama is the story of Jesus, who lived the highest and most successful life ever. It disclosed the triumph of God's plan that included both humanity's grievous failure at the Cross and Spirit's supreme triumph in the Resurrection.

The great drama and stirring adventure in Paul's life was the spiritual transformation of Saul into Paul. The defeats were part of the metamorphosis—and fortunately for Paul, many of the aspects of Saul did fail! What Saul *was* succumbed to what Paul *became*—the ancient teaching of the way of the spiritual path.

Through his magnificent defeats, Paul learned what Jesus meant when he said: " . . . *the Son can do nothing of his own accord . . . .*" (John 5:19) This Scripture is really another wonderful promise: We do not have to overcome or attain anything alone. We are never stuck where we are. Because, if we allow it, the Christ Spirit that indwells us can come alive in us as an undefeatable, all-victorious transforming power for God's plan and purpose for each of us. This is what Paul came to realize after some very lonely, discouraging, and wretched experiences. *I can do all things in him who strengthens me.* (Phil. 4:13)

This gave Paul the insight we all need into the relative frontier between failure and success. God can work His great plans and purposes through both. All true success comes from Him, from finding and following His divine plan of good for our lives. And the only real failure is when we neglect to do what God's plan requires from us.

God's plan is often surprising. The way of spiritual transformation and growth is often surprising. Paul once reminded the Corinthians: *But, as it is written, "What no eye has seen, nor ear heard, nor the heart of man conceived, what God has prepared for those who love him, . . . "* (I Cor. 2:9)

This is the great drama of uncertainty concerning what lies ahead in the pathway of spiritual growth.

Paul, reminiscing about his new life after the Damascus Road turning point, wrote that he had been lashed, beaten, stoned, snakebitten, and shipwrecked. He further elaborated on being in danger of rivers, robbers, strangers, his own people, cities, wilderness, and false brothers. He suffered toil, hardship, sleepless nights, hunger, thirst, and daily pressure and anxiety about others and himself. Yet he understood and affirmed: *I consider that the sufferings of this present time are not worth comparing with the glory that is to be revealed to us.* (Romans 8:18)

When we learn what Paul learned, we shall see that it is no longer a question of failure or success, but whether we are following and fulfilling God's plan for us. Life successfully lived is a creative partnership in which (in Jesus' words): *" . . . My Father is working still, and I am working."* (John 5:17)

In Unity, we know that our most important work is done in consciousness. It is often hard work to hold thoughts and feelings that are conducive to spiritual transformation and growth. It is also in our thoughts and feelings that we experience most of our hardships, persecutions, humiliations, and abuses.

But all that is required of us is to do the best we can—at any time—and not berate ourselves or others about mistakes and defeats. A Chinese, Wan Yong Ming, once said: *The great virtue of man lies in his abilities to correct his mistakes and to continually make a new man of himself.* Paul recognized the even higher truth that when we use our human abilities to uplift and refine our consciousness, we open ourselves to a mighty spiritual reinforcement.

It always helps to see what someone else has done in rising above defeat, loss, and heartbreak. It is inspiring to know about others who, with God's help, have transmuted handicaps and mistakes into magnificent victories.

In my own life, I used to dwell on regrets; but now, as I reminisce, I find that God has been working things together for good beyond anything I ever planned. And the life of the great Apostle is a classic example of how victory can swallow up all defeat when we, as he, make the all-important discovery that *For me to live is Christ, . . .* (Phil. 1:21) and then following through with *. . . I press on toward the goal for the prize of the upward call of God in Christ Jesus.* (Phil. 3:4)

Continuing Guidance

Exploring the Bible for its great dramas introduces us to the great drama of life itself; for truly, the Bible is a library of life, with issues and interests that sweep through every corner of humanity. Its intrigue lies not only in the past but in the present and the future. At all times and under all circumstances the Bible can be . . . *a lamp to my feet and a light to my path.* (Psalms 119:105) It can be a constant guide.

The Bible is the most instructive history that we possess. It gives example after example of both the right and wrong uses of the principles and laws that are forever with us to guide us to the highest life and greatest good for all.

The Bible can help us train and govern our ability to make moment-by-moment choices that lead upward and onward in the Godward path of life.

Even more, the spiritual Truth that abounds in Scripture can quicken in us the timeless illumination and guidance that come from the source of infinite intelligence within ourselves.

Much of the great drama of our lives is that ordinarily we live in the awareness of an ever-advancing time slot we call "now." We know (if we remember) everything that has occurred in the past—right up to this moment—but we know nothing for certain about what is to come, even in the very next minute. Yet everything in life is headed forward into the great unknown. Still, the biblical promise holds: . . . *He will be our guide for ever.* (Psalms 48:14)

Every great character in the Bible became great by learning to receive and obey the guidance of that mysterious inner Teacher that guides us to all Truth, the Christ within that . . . *enlightens every man* . . . . (John 1:9)

The apostle Paul was given one of the most startling introductions to the living Christ in history. We have much to learn from the ensuing drama in Paul's extraordinary life. We have already explored the remarkable outer experiences and adventures in the amazing difference between what he was as Saul, a well-educated, wealthy, high-ranking Jew, and what he became as Paul, without his worldly estate, but in possession of a new quality of existence and under the government and operation of spiritual forces and creative powers that had been totally unknown and inaccessible in his old way of life. Paul had needed to release and die to many possessions of the past, and then face new, often unexpected challenges and perils. But there were no regrets. Paul summed up his appreciation, his gratitude, his joy, his reverence for the magnificence of his new life with the declaration: *For to me to live is*

Christ, and to die is gain. (Phil. 1:21)

Let's return and explore the guiding forces that had evolved Saul into the new man, Paul. Originally his education had given him the command and control of a well-developed intellect. In addition, Saul had the advantage of good religious training, centered in the Torah, the Mosaic code of life. He had become intensely devoted to the pursuit of right living through understanding and obedience to the law, which was based on the Yahweh concept of God as Lord or Law.

Law, rightly understood and used, can be a trusted guide in many things. For example, working with electricity, flying an airplane, or thinking positive, creative thoughts. But, in religion, the tendency was and still is to fix attention on outward observances. In Saul's day, Jewish observance of law was almost entirely external, with laws for every tiny detail of behavior in Jewish life: what to eat, drink, wear, whom to associate with, whom to marry, how to do and not to do nearly everything in life. And, as Jesus poignantly pointed out, life based on effects rather than causes tends to produce a sepulcher-like life, embellished on the outside, but unwholesome, corrupt, and degenerate within. In fact, the only human trait Jesus openly attacked was the religious attitudes and approach characterized by the Pharisees—the self-righteous fundamentalists of

His day—of regulating externals, judging, arbitrating rules and conduct of others, and using the law as a weapon of restraint and control, while remaining, inside, whitewashed tombs themselves! Jesus revealed that the tendency to do the former almost certainly indicates the latter—a deadly error in spiritual growth.

Because of his Pharisaical background, Paul arbitrated a great many rules to others in his effort to build an ecclesiastic constituency. But as he grew in spiritual understanding he learned to apply law rightly—where it counts and serves best as a trusted and dependable guide—within himself. Paul learned to work with the law of mind action, applying the dynamics of creative law to the causative process of right thinking and feeling, which produces right conduct and right living (. . . *think about these things*). (Phil. 4:8) Paul had learned, as Jesus had taught, that the law is not a restricting, suppressing constraint, but a benevolent guardian influence that guides and leads us ever higher into the expression of spiritual Truth and the ultimate expression of Spirit-love.

Paul learned that love fulfills all law, not by setting it aside or rendering it inactive, but by working all things together for the good. Spiritual fulfillment is attained by the law of growth and development. As each level is fulfilled according to the law of that stage of development, it is transmuted into a higher level under the operation of the law at that level. Each level adds its increase, and love, as a creative synthesis, always adds new qualities of its own.

For us, it is a matter of consciousness. The creative process of the universe (the one we read about in Genesis) works through our own thoughts and feelings. And as we evolve in consciousness into higher and higher awareness, and release more and more of our inherent spiritual qualities, we continue to operate under the law of mind action. And in any level of consciousness, much of our good and dependable guidance comes to us through the ordinary application of a continuing basic law—positive thinking!

Does it sound too simple? Positive thinking, in itself, has no power. But positive thoughts open us to a great power. Our thoughts build the frame and support of the world we experience. Positive thoughts are uplifting, encouraging, and constructive thoughts. They tend to foster feelings of optimism, creativity, peace, forgiveness, and love. They tend to rise above the limitations and destructiveness of negativity. They build an attitude—a direction in consciousness—that points us Godward. They open us to inspiration and the activity of the Holy Spirit. Positive thoughts, together with positive feelings, nurture and sponsor all the constructive attributes and creative activities that fulfill the principle of our being (I Am) according to the law of our being *(" . . . the way, and the truth, and the life . . . ").* (John 14:6)

Part of guidance lies, first, in correction. When our thoughts and feelings begin to pull us in an unhappy, unhealthy, unproductive direction, nothing has greater power to turn us toward the Father and put us together again than prayer and meditation.

Prayers are usually conceived in terms of needs and requests. They are usually problem-oriented. Meditation involves us more in a passive stillness, which detaches and releases us from our current earth-life concerns. It induces a different state of consciousness than that in which we ordinarily live our lives. It stills the intellect, rests the five senses, and tends to translate our material desires into their spiritual equivalent. It is like the prodigal son's trip home, in which the "lost" part of our unexpressed spiritual nature is found. In meditation we discover and release our latent divine heritage. Meditation is less an exercise of words than an experience in receptivity and "flow."

Both prayer and meditation are agents for inner growth and soul enlargement. The important changes occur in us. When we are truly open and receptive in our prayer life, we are often given new goals and new awareness of our own qualities and capacities to grow into them. Answers, which can either come to us "on the dead run" or in the beautiful, peaceful depths of inner silence, usually come to us—all so simply—as ideas.

Charles Fillmore said that our divine heritage from God comes to us in the form of ideas. An idea is like a seed. It contains everything needed for its fulfillment except, like a seed, the right soil, nourishment, and cultivation. Ideas are free, immortal, and they are (again like seeds) centers of creativity. They can sometimes cause us a little pain, or they can exalt us; above all, they can be great forces for our good. Indeed, *nothing is as powerful as an idea whose time has come.* And the right time is often determined by the quality and receptivity of our consciousness.

Perhaps now we can more appreciate the immense value that an idea can be to us and the importance of positive thinking in establishing the right context.

Prayers are often answered by our simply receiving an idea, an idea that we are to put to work and use in our lives, but an idea that probably would not have come to us if we had not prayed. God also guides us through the association of ideas.

For example, if you decided to pray for a better garden than you had last year, you would be wise to recognize as guidance the idea of adding the right ingredients to make the soil more fertile. In most prayers, the answer comes through us, and it enriches us in the process.

So we see that the two most common ways that God has provided for our guidance through life is through the right application of His dependable laws and the constructive use of His ideas. In my own life, when things get complicated and seem uncertain, I have found that my surest guidance—and the simplest ideas to follow—come by asking only for the next step. I have been amazed how clear and simple it has been to understand and follow through the very next thing at hand; whereas, at times, the long-range contemplation would have disconcerted or even overwhelmed me. (There is a great deal of mastery and guidance at our command in living one step, one day at a time.)

The clearest idea ever given to us about how life is to be lived—at all times—is found in the life and teachings of Jesus. He came to reveal the spiritual Truth about life. In its essence, the Jesus Christ Truth can be best understood in terms of ideas, divine ideas "made flesh."

In writing about his . . . *visions and revelations of the Lord* (II Cor. 12:1), Paul connected this glorious experience with his thorn in the flesh. It may well have been that the thorn was the constant aggravation from the "orthodox" Apostles about Paul having never personally known Jesus.

They used this fact with Paul often, and he countered by claiming in the beginning of his Epistles that he was . . . called to be an apostle of Jesus Christ, not through the ways of men, but spiritually! This is an all-important lesson that we can learn from Paul; this is a wonderful example of what Jesus meant by worshipping " . . . *in spirit and truth.*" (John 4:24) This is the message of Jesus. He came to disclose the Christ (crystalline) ideas of the spiritual Truth about life, " . . . *the way, and the truth, and the life . . .*" (John 14:6) of coming to the Father through the inner path of spiritual guidance and growth.

Once the message of Jesus is understood spiritually, it becomes the essence of simplicity itself: God is our spiritual Father; we are His spiritual children, and His spiritual nature is vested in us as our spiritual heritage—a waiting kingdom of latent spiritual potential that progressively unfolds from within as we grow into our spiritual maturity (just as a tree unfolds toward fruition from its seed). Spiritual growth is accompanied in every phase of development (according to the plan of good in the seed) by spiritual guidance.

So far, we have observed the ways God can guide us through our ordinary ways of thinking. But there is also a higher process. The more we uplift our minds with positive thoughts and fill them with spiritual Truth, the more receptive we are to the influence of a quality of direct knowing that transcends the limits of our current intellect and word knowledge, and awakens us to higher realms of consciousness (the kingdom of heaven). This spiritual revealment is the intuition that inspired all the great characters of the Bible as well as poets, artists, inventors, great scientists, mystics, geniuses—all the creative thinkers of history whose visions and revelations have advanced mankind all along the way. This profound personal experience validates spiritual Truth beyond intellectual doubt. It is the guide to all Truth. No wonder Paul felt so strongly about the authenticity and authority of his spiritual apostleship of the living Christ.

This illumined guidance does not come by command. But each of our minds contains the gift of an ability to achieve heightened consciousness and grow into the access of our heritage of God's infinite intelligence. (. . . *we have the mind of Christ.*) (I Cor. 2:16) The discipline of right thinking and the beautiful "still waters" of deep meditation cultivate our gift of higher consciousness. They attune and sensitize us to the constant, loving whisper of God's . . . *still small voice* (I Kings 19:12) within us.

The dwelling place of all Truth is within ourselves. From here—the Christ within—God reveals and gives Himself into our lives. . . . *it is the Spirit himself bearing witness with our spirit that we are children of God, and if children, then heirs, heirs of God and fellow heirs with Christ . . . .* (Romans 8:16, 17)

As did Paul, accept that your main job is to keep your thoughts and feelings positive, loving, and full of Truth. *Do your best to present yourself to God as one approved, a workman who has no need to be ashamed, rightly handling the word of truth.* (II Timothy 2:15) And then, cultivate a sense of His ever-abiding presence with and in you. Expect His guidance! Know that God already knows the answer to anything you need to know. And you will learn, as Paul did, about the *. . . secret and hidden wisdom of God . . . :* (I Cor. 2:7) *"What no eye has seen, nor ear heard, nor the heart of man conceived, what God has prepared for those who love Him," God has revealed to us through the Spirit.* (I Cor. 2:9)

The Ultimate Plan

We now arrive at the final and most climactic drama of the Bible, the book Revelation (the Revelation of John the Divine). This remarkable piece of literature has not been an easy book for the Western mind to understand. By its very nature, it is not to be taken literally, and it is safe to say that no other book has had such divergent and controversial interpretation.

Revelation is one of two books in the Bible known as apocalyptic literature (the other is the book of Daniel in the Old Testament). Apocalypse means to reveal what has been hidden away and kept secret. The word *secret* gives us a clue to a meaningful understanding of this extraordinary book, which is permeated by strange, baffling, mystical, and veiled symbology. Indeed, any reader who does not understand the deeper intention behind the peculiar and often bizarre imagery of Eastern apocalyptic literature will be at a loss to understand its real meaning. They, in fact, may fall into the very trap that was set for all but the initiate.

This brings us to the original purpose for which the book was written. The growing number of early Christians, many of them Gentiles and pagans, provoked a full scale persecution against all Christians (there were eventually ten Imperial persecutions in which many were beaten, crucified, and burned). The followers of Jesus Christ were driven underground and became a loosely organized secret society. It even became punishable by death to possess Christian literature.

The initial purpose of this apocalypse was to convey a secret message of encouragement that would be unintelligible, or a diversion to any oppressor who might read them. In other words, the form of Revelation is that of a cryptogram—a secret message that needs to be properly decoded.

The book itself was only gradually accepted by the canon of the early church—and it remained controversial as late as the Reformation—yet it has been responsible for a considerable part of the so-called fundamentalist doctrine that has made Christianity a heavy, guilt-obsessed, intrusive religion. (As we move toward the underlying message of Revelation, it would be good to remind ourselves of the qualities Paul listed as . . . *the fruit of Spirit* . . . (Gal. 5:22) and recognize that the only mark of a true Christian is how much Christ shines through.)

So again, it is well to remember that the very purpose of the book of Revelation was to convey a hidden, secret message to those who would know the mysterious symbology and to conceal it from all those who would not. To gain the real message we must seek the hidden meaning and not press for Western literal understanding.

The message of Revelation is dispatched in the form of a forecast and aimed at one of humanity's deepest needs—the promise of deliverance. (And the message is for the whole of humanity; any exclusiveness disappears for those who have *"ears to hear."*)

Behind and beyond the original reason for writing this apocalypse was inspired a far greater perception. Some regard this as futuristic, and all along the way, even with the obvious symbology, a literal interpretation of "the end of the world" has been applied to various historical crises—so-called signs of the last days. This included events involving certain popes, Luther, Napoleon, the Kaiser, Hitler, Stalin, Mao, the youth rebellion, and the declining morals of America. But history itself keeps postponing these interpretations (a bit embarrassing for the predictors, but at least allowing a little more time to use fear as a pulpit device to recruit and control more converts). Each person's world is his perception. It ends with a new awareness—a process that can seem very distressing to old, entrenched concepts and resistant feelings.

The predictions will become accurate when they are always current, realizing that *every day is*

Judgment Day, and that the message does not concern a specific historical situation but has a timeless, up-to-the-minute interpretation about our present level of individual as well as collective spiritual development.

Revelation is the Bible's cabalistic presentation of the Gospel of Jesus. It reveals the same "good news," the same hidden truth that was behind the teachings, parables, miracles, and the life of Jesus—the Word made flesh. (Spiritual teachings live by symbols; their deeper meaning can be conveyed no other way). The message of Jesus is " . . . *the way, and the truth, and the life . . .* " (John 14:6) of attaining spiritual union with God. Revelation unveils the deeper esoteric meaning of the spiritual unfoldment of humanity, showing what happens as we evolve along the path. It discloses the ultimate plan for attaining . . . *the goal for the prize of the upward call of God in Christ Jesus.* (Phil. 3:14) The mystery of Revelation is the same mystery that Paul disclosed in Colossians 1:25-27: . . . . *to make the word of God fully known, the mystery hidden for ages . . . which is Christ in you, the hope of glory.*

Revelation is: *The Revelation of Jesus Christ, which God gave him to show to his servants what must soon take place; . . . for the time is near.* (Rev. 1:1, 3) The time is always near. Jesus began His ministry with the pronouncement:

" . . . the kingdom of heaven is at hand." (Matthew 4:17) Truth is forever. The promise of Jacob's vision is that on the ladder of life, God forever meets us wherever we are. As we enter the pathway of spiritual regeneration, the promise is even more encouraging: Each step of our ever-changing needs will be fulfilled by the awesome power of spiritual transformation.

So the truth of John's Revelation—shrouded in mystery and clothed in the symbolism of striking and often highly wrought imagery, visionary figures and settings, vivid, dramatic, pictorial presentations of conflict, mythology, numerology—is the eternal verity about our hope of glory: the evolving stages of our human development, life's ever-present opportunities for our growth, the inner conflicts, growing pains and dark nights of the soul in the overcoming process, and the ultimate triumph of God's Spirit in us. It ends with a beautiful vision of the ultimate destiny of the world—heaven on earth.

Let's follow some of Revelation's symbology and get a feel for its message. The prologue of the drama gives us a visionary introduction to the *son of man* (God in man), and centers us first in a symbolic picture of the qualities of Christhood seen in Jesus Christ: *seven golden lampstands* (spiritual illumination), *a long robe* and *golden girdle* (priestly symbols of holiness, wholeness, completeness), *white hair, eyes like a flame of fire* (age-old symbols of wisdom and spiritual perspective), *feet like burnished bronze* (stability of a spiritual foundation), *seven stars in his right hand* (the authority of divine sonship in heaven and on Earth), *two-edged sword* (the sword of spiritual truth, the power of the spoken word of truth), *the Alpha and Omega — the first and the last* (the eternal I AM nature of the Christ that lives within).

The first act of the seven-act drama consists of a series of seven visions based on letters to seven churches in Asia [Minor]. These symbolize rungs on the ladder of our unfoldment, with a review of their special challenges and a divine remedy for each (the overcoming principles to use in various areas of our own consciousness). Each calls for a drastic change in attitudes. The acts do not necessarily progress in chronological order, but each (the seven seals, the seven trumpets, the three great portents, the seven plagues, the overthrow of Babylon, and the new heaven and Earth) is a powerful, fantastic expression (often amazingly applicable to the psychological activities of our subconscious) of the road map to New Jerusalem.

Numbers are important symbols (borrowed from the traditions of the cabala—the Jewish mystery literature). Seven, which is used so often, refers to stages of fulfillment in the world of phenomena. Three symbolizes heaven—as in the

Trinity; four represents Earth. Their total, seven, as in the days of creation, is the blending and synthesis of levels of fulfillment in our Earth life. Twelve means spiritual fulfillment (essential within—such as the spiritualized expression of our twelve faculties of soul). Thus, twelve times twelve equals 144, the multiplying power of spiritual influence; adding three zeroes (144,000) symbolizes the infinite intelligence available to Christ consciousness.

There are many other symbols in Revelation: a lamb, four horses, beasts and dragons, the throne of God, sickles, stars, gates, hidden manna, a woman and child, Hades, the river of the water of life, the bride, and the bright and morning star. Two symbols are given particular emphasis by doomsday religionists, the Antichrist (the denying of sonship), and the war of Armageddon (the inner battleground in the war of concepts and ideologies).

The massive information in Revelation is more than almost anyone can assimilate, but it stands as a body of Truth, ready to unveil life's spiritual secrets in all its vistas.

Generally, Revelation can be applied as an encouragement to remain faithful to the high vision of Jesus Christ, to trust Spirit and its process, to believe in the power of Christ in our lives, in spite of all appearances, to know that given "a crack of willingness" the Spirit of God in us can transform our lives even when we sometimes succumb to the false teachings that deny the Christ within and cleave to the temporal power of the outer manifest world. The breath of spring in the often outlandish and enigmatic motif of Eastern apocalyptic writing is the clear statement: *"Behold, I make all things new."* (Rev. 21:5) And in God's universal plan of good, no door ever closes, no world ever ends, but that there is a newer, better one ready and waiting.

The last act of Revelation uses another beautiful image to depict the wondrous glory (which means to experience the awareness of God's presence) of the realized kingdom, the New Jerusalem—spiritualized consciousness—and its ultimate triumph over all that has manifested less than good.

Now as always in our Earth life experience of learning and growing, we must increasingly look away from all the old Jerusalem of material bondage to the New Jerusalem of the life from Spirit within.

The basic law of life is progress. It does not have to be painful if we remember that the old order changes, giving place to new; thus God fulfills Himself.

He Is Risen

I invite you now to join me in a little journey back in time two thousand years to the Sunday that has come to be known as Easter, and to share in the experience of one of the most joyous and poignant stories of all time.

It started that morning in sorrow when Mary Magdalene arrived brokenhearted at the tomb of Jesus simply to complete the traditional Jewish burial rites. The Easter story had really begun the week before with the triumphal entry of Jesus into Jerusalem—in His great decision to face the powers of that time. Then followed the dramatic, intense experience of that original Holy Week. Jesus met with the disciples in the Upper Room where they shared the Last Supper, where He had told them many things, most of which they only began to understand much later.

Eventually, there was the hour of Gethsemane, where Jesus experienced the Crucifixion, the Resurrection, and the Ascension of His consciousness. There was the mockery of a trial and the Crucifixion between two thieves (which some say represent the past and the future, and others merely the struggling nature of our human point of view).

Then there was the quiet time of the tomb, in

which Jesus lay in creative rest, but which symbolized to His followers that apparently everything had collapsed around them. For they at that time had no awareness of Easter and the Resurrection that would come, and they grieved deeply because the man they thought would lead them into a heaven on Earth had turned out to be "mortal," and had died on a cross. All of their hopes and dreams had died too, and they withdrew in abandon.

Because a corpse could not be touched on the Sabbath, Jesus' remains were hastily laid in a borrowed tomb with a great stone rolled in front of it to prevent the body from being stolen. It was the first possible moment—at the break of dawn—that Mary Magdalene arrived at the grave, not to greet her risen Lord, but to pour embalming oil on His body. She was distressed to find that the stone had been rolled away and the tomb was empty. She wept and poured out her concern about the missing body to the "gardener," whom we now know was really Jesus. When she at last recognized Him and recovered somewhat, He sent her to tell the disciples the most astounding and best news of all time.

Jesus had mentioned His Resurrection all through His ministry, and He had raised three others from the grave. But apparently the tragedy of the Crucifixion had completely driven this from their minds, and none of them expected to greet their risen Lord. The proof of Jesus' Resurrection is substantial, and the historical evidence is well established, far more, for example, than the assassination of Caesar. But nowhere is the effect of the Resurrection more simply and wonderfully seen than in the renewal of His own followers when He appeared to them and they learned that what Jesus had previously said had meant an actual Resurrection—a raising of the body and soul after human death.

The day He was crucified He had only a few followers. It was the Resurrection that gave the early church its enormous drive, vitality, courage, hope, and growth.

Jesus Christ is actually more alive today than He was before His death. He influences far more people; He is better understood; He is more inspiring and comforting. The world has never been the same since His Resurrection.

Easter morning flung open the "windows of life" toward the omnipotence, omniscience, and omnipresence of God's nature, and it assured us of the infinite potential and power that support and preserve all the good in God's creation. As science has recently uncovered the staggering forces at the heart of nature, far more overwhelming are the mighty spiritual forces that Jesus revealed at Easter.

Jesus was able to identify Himself with the spirit, the principles, the purposes, and the power within all life. If we can share any part of this identity, if we can but glimpse our lives in their eternal context, resurrection will happen to us! There will be for us an Easter insight, a real contact with the living Christ, a change, a new beginning, a new dimension of life filled with vibrant, living power, goodness, and love. Easter has not yet happened to most people. For most, the three-dimensional world of fact is still the only reality. We have been trained to believe in the supreme dominion of facts and the eternal Truths of Easter are rarely experienced. So when someone does experience Easter as a spiritual reality, it is a rare and beautiful thing.

Resurrection was part of the total message that Jesus came to reveal about us, which is that we are majestic beings who have but to know our own spiritual nature and to work and give ourselves over entirely to becoming what we were intended to be. The whole purpose of existence is growth and expansion into fulfillment. Every atom in the universe (which we now know can yield unbelievable power) embodies but one idea—to express itself into fullness—and so with us. We are here to learn and to grow spiritually. As God's image, we have been placed here to do just that! To " . . . *be perfect as your heavenly Father is perfect."* (Matt. 5:48) We unfold our divine potential by conquering and overcoming all that within ourselves that is less than what we can be, and with the power of Spirit, we are raised up into new levels of consciousness and to inevitable new possibilities of expression.

How can children of God not want to be victorious in becoming what they were created to be? Easter says that nothing can defeat the divine pattern that is within us. Easter is the perennial reminder of the potential of resurrection that is incorporated into all life. Resurrection can be understood as part of the divine pattern of nature itself, an integral influence in the upward, onward path of spiritual evolution and spiritual unfoldment. The very essence of the Easter message is to call forth the new.

Easter is the celebration of the risen Christ that makes all things new. It is a historical event and it is a disclosure of a deathless Source behind all life. It is an affirmation that the right kind of life is worth it, because anything good that you establish in your life is yours forever. Easter means that the worst has been met and conquered—that death itself is but a new beginning, a doorway into larger life.

But Easter is also something more! The "Treasure" of Easter is timeless, the eternal significance is always new. Easter is not for Jesus alone. Easter can be a very personal, intimate, spiritual experience for each individual; for Christ lives in us. We too can rise!

Each of us now probably has entombed hopes, dreams, longings, opportunities, and divine possibilities that have been crucified and buried, things that very much need resurrecting. Easter is a spiritual opportunity to resurrect all these things. Contained within the Resurrection message is the promise that you can have a glimpse of the eternal magnificence of that soul of yours and stir into life something that is larger and fuller than you have ever known before.

Wouldn't it be marvelous if you did resurrect an old hope, dream, or longing into a new vision, a new interest, a new purpose, a new dedication? Wouldn't it be great if you were to roll away the stone and be delivered from your disillusions and really feel forgiven, unburdened, accepted, like graduation to a higher level of life?

Let's see how it can best happen. First, remember life is consciousness, lived within out, ever evolving into higher and fuller awareness. The story of Easter is really the story of the entry into the kind of life that is found in Christ consciousness. It is the life that Jesus lived. Science has found that the resurrection of the mind and heart does marvelous things for the body (and I might add for our surroundings and relationships). Because it must come first in our consciousness, it helps immensely when we begin lifting our thoughts out of old tombs into eternal Truth. We can begin by denying the validity of our doubts about God's power in our lives and affirming our ever-present accessibility to His indwelling spiritual reinforcement. Remember, with God all things are possible. It helps to recall all the good that has happened to us in the past, which will make us more aware of how often God does help us. Every time we think thoughts about Christ, Christ is raised again in us. Reverence is also a big part of the Easter "feeling"—reverence for the nature of God, reverence for the life and triumph of Jesus, and reverence for that lovable, striving, conquering spirit in us.

We are transformed by the renewing of our minds. This is our part: maintaining a positive, affirmative state of mind. Truth will then resurrect in our consciousness, and things will begin to happen.

The Crucifixion and the Resurrection were steps that led to the Ascension. Jesus Christ ascended so that He could be with every man, woman, and child forever. He lives, not in some distant heaven, but here and now. He is not "coming," He is here now, within each of us, loving, helping, inspiring, lifting, raising each of us anytime we open our minds and hearts to Him.

After Jesus Christ was risen from the dead He said: " . . . lo, I am with you always . . . ." (Matt. 28:20) Anytime, anywhere, and in whatever way we need Him, the spiritual presence of the living Christ is with us. When we become conscious of His presence, we awaken in us His likeness. The greatest need of humankind today is for Christ to be resurrected in us. Let us join together in a prayer experience in which we invoke and invite His nature to rise up through ours, and let us remember that whatever Truth we now feel, anything that we now establish in our lives, is ours forever—from now through eternity.

Father, we turn in consciousness to the recognition of Your abiding presence and of our oneness with You, and we give thanks that You have been, and are now our Guide and Preceptor, our "very present help," revealing to us the transcending power of Your Spirit in the inward Self of us—that makes Easter very real to us. As we accept the consciousness of resurrection, we open ourselves to Your resurrecting power, and we thank You for the joy of knowing that Truth is eternal and that a life centered in Truth can be lived in abundance and peace. Father, let the resurrecting, overcoming, perfecting power of the Spirit of Christ take over in our hearts and flow forth through us. We give thanks that the same Spirit that raised Jesus from death is here now, raising us into high levels of spiritual consciousness and giving us new life, inspiration, growth, and Christ expression. Because He lives, we too shall live. The stones of old limitations shall be rolled away, and we are made new in mind, body, and spirit.

Printed U.S.A.
157-F-5570-15M-7-82